C000051100

Just A Thought - Stories from a Baby-Boomers Life

Just A Thought - Stories from a Baby-Boomers Life

Stories from a Baby-Boomers Life

Andy Smith

TKR Publishing
Nashville, TN

copyright 2019 TKR Publishing Nashville, TN all rights reserved

Cover by Berta Martinez * Author photos by Tom Hamilton

Contents

Note To Readers

If you are an English teacher, a Literature teacher or a person of very strict grammar expectations when reading a book, PLEASE put this book down and get your money back!

If you feel lead to send me an email to point out your horror of reading my stories with such horrible paragraph structure, PLEASE understand that I am retired and have plenty of time to send you a constant flow of hateful emails that will make Donald Trump tweets sound like Mother Teresa.

When I wrote my column, Just A Thought, I was a slave to perfect grammar and paragraph structure. Every column was 2 pages, 6-800 words and perfectly styled in what any English teacher could appreciate.

When I put together this book, I threw away the English book.

It's called JUST A THOUGHT, so I approached my editing skills (in which I have NONE) into a structure of thoughts, not paragraphs.

It almost has a poetic rhythm feel to it, I'm thinking.

If the structure of the stories bothers you, read something else.

I will not apologize.

I was going for the rhythm of the story, not the proper structure.

Introduction

During the last millennium, my grandfather, Paul Gerard Smith, had a column named SMITHEREENS that ran in small local papers. As a successful screenwriter, director and playwright, SMITHEREENS was a nice platform for Grandpa to take a break and simply speak his mind. The columns were never serious and had no particular theme or agenda.

If you look around my family tree, you'll find several column writers on the Smith side.

My great-grandfather, Carlton Smith, was the first syndicated columnist in America.

In fact, you can follow the family tree all the way back to Ireland (on my fathers side) and find nothing but creative writers.

Well I certainly couldn't let my branch of the family tree grow without its own leaves, could I?

Besides, I was a budding songwriter and my column served as a nice break from all the rhyming, syllables and rhythmic patterns built in creating a threeminute song.

I started where my grandpa left off, writing SMITHEREENS for my generation.

I was quickly reminded by my daughters, however, that there was a Rock 'N Roll band by the same name and it might behoove me to rename my wordily contributions.

So I came up with JUST A THOUGHT because after all, that's all the column was about.

My column never made a big splash on the journalistic front. It ran in a few 'fish wrappers', as we writers like to call them, but editors of these small town papers are notorious for breaking the rhythm of a column by using them as 'fillers' which goes a long way in killing the continuity needed to develop a loyal following.

But I was okay with that.

Like my grandfather before me, my column was more of a break from the other, more serious projects that I was working on and I enjoyed every opportunity to sit down and spit out another edition of JUST A THOUGHT.

What I liked about my column is that it broke the standard rules of column writing in today's world.

Any successful column writer is identified with a specific topic. Your column is about politics, family, sports, religion – your column has a specific voice that the reader can count on every day when they snap open their paper.

But I have never looked at people or life as one-dimensional.

Diversity has always been the one element in this life that I celebrate the most.

The more one dimensional a person is, the less interested I am in dealing with them.

Sure, I could have written a column about fatherhood and probably done quite well. But why shelve all the great opinions I have about sports, religion, politics and nothing in particular?

The schooled journalist would say that my column doesn't have a voice and that is why it is not successful.

I say it does have a voice – MY voice – and I will use that voice for whatever random thoughts I may be having at the time, thank you very much.

So whether I'm trying to figure out how pioneers got by without alarm clocks or comparing a Jimmi Hendrix concert to taking my kid to the doctors, solving the problems of elections or trying to stay up to modern technology, my column had a voice – my voice – and I was always happy to share it with anyone who happened to come by.

It was never intended to change the world or make any great impact.

It was simply meant to be: JUST A THOUGHT.

The author

Main Body

When I Refuse to Die

I think I've figured out why I'm going to live to be 100 years old. No it has nothing to do with abstinence from alcohol and cigarettes. I have no idea what my cholesterol level is or my blood pressure. I have no appetite for bland, cardboard tasting cereals, and I don't even want to talk about my physical fitness routines.

I will live to be 100 years old because of pure stubbornness.

Simply put, I refuse to die until they do something to make death more reasonable for a guy like me.

Now I will say that I have been a pretty lucky guy up to this point. I haven't been to a funeral since the '60s. In fact, the only funerals I've been to for family has been when grandmas and grandpas have quietly slipped away into the hereafter after a nice, long, healthy life. With five brothers and sisters and tons of aunts, uncles, nieces and nephews, cousins and whatnot, I think that's a pretty good gene pool.

But I have looked into this final chapter in our journeys and I can say flat out that I refuse to die until they make some changes around here.

I was talking to a friend of mine who works at a mortuary. I was telling him that I thought I might die sometime in my lifetime, preferably towards the end, although writers have been known to die more often than cats so it all becomes a mute point for writers anyway. Well I wanted to know what I could expect from the good people who would be letting me down for the last time.

"Well," he tells me, "To begin with, we'll have to embalm you."

"Embalm me?!?"... I can tell by the sound of the word that I don't think this is something I want done to me.

"What does embalming do for me?!?" I ask.

"It preserves you... so you don't turn into a pile of dust so quickly." Then he continues in a tone of boastfulness, "Why if we do a good enough job, they can take you out of the ground ten years later and you would look good as new!"

I look at my friend with a pained look. This doesn't sound so great to me.

"Well I'll have to let them know that they don't need to embalm me. Ain't nobody going to want to dig me up after I'm gone. No need for the family to waste any money on such unimportant stuff like that. You know, ashes to ashes, dust to dust... that will work fine for me, thanks."

"But you don't have any say in the matter. You'll have to be embalmed. It's the law, you know." He says a bit miffed that I should turn my nose at such an efficient service.

"Hey," I protest," I was into natural birth, so why can't I have a natural death, huh?!? Besides, I've been fighting preservatives all my life in chips and dips, and now you're telling me that you guys are going to load me up with the stuff after I die anyway? GetOuttaHere!!?"

"Sorry." he says with a smile that tells me the case is closed.

"Now," he continues, "You might want to select your casket, burial plot and type of service you want beforehand. It's a lot easier on the loved ones, you know."

"Well it would probably be a lot easier for me, too." I say, "So here's what I want." I say, as my friend braces himself. "I just want to be buried in a simple pine box... nothing fancy for me. Hey, I'll even supply the wood for ya. I don't want them putting me in some big limousine... I never rode in one when I was alive, I sure as hell don't want to when I'm dead and can't enjoy the bar that comes with it. I don't want them putting any expensive suits on me. I was always more comfortable in Hawaiian shirts and jeans, you know. You can bury me wherever you want, but hey, if you don't mind, I think it would be cool if they buried me under the street on Broadway in New York City... I've always said I wanted to end up on Broadway. As for the service, well nothing too cheesy for me, thank you. Some beer and peanuts would be nice, but tell people not to wear black... it's so depressing looking. And please, no wordy speeches that make me sound like a saint. If you can't say those things to me when I'm alive, then there's no need to waste your breath when I'm dead. Read some of my stories, play some of my songs... you know, just to let them know that I've left something behind."

I sit back refreshed, feeling as if I've got this dying thing all figured out.

My friend looks a bit dazed, however.

"Well," he says with hesitation, "I hate to be the spoiler, but it doesn't quite work that way. You can't be buried in a pine box. There are regulations, you know. You have to use the cars that we provide. Insurance you understand. They'll want you to wear a suit out of respect, you know. And you'll have to be buried in a licensed cemetery. But I suppose the service could be whatever you want it to be." He concludes with a fragile smile.

I stand up indignant, "Yea, well, let me tell you buster, if I can't go out the way I want to, then by God, I refuse to die!"

Case closed.

Not So Wise Men

One of the greatest contradictions in the Bible is in reference to the three wise men. If these guys were wise, then I would have been a flat out genius had I been hanging around in those days.

Now I realize that time has a way of washing down historical events, leaving much to our imaginations. All we get some 2000 years later is that these three kings who were wise came to bring gifts to the baby Jesus and forgot to go back and tell Herod before they headed back to their kingdoms, so Herod killed a bunch of two year old boys.

It's anyone's guess as to where they came from – we are told they traveled several months.

We don't know much about what kind of kings they were.

We don't know what distinguished them as 'wise'.

And we don't know who the idiot was who brought the Myrrh – go ahead, look it up. Myrrh was a perfume used in those days for funerals. How 'wise' did that guy feel when he got there and realized it was a baby shower, not a funeral. Sure glad he wasn't the ruler of MY kingdom!

But that's not the story.

All through the story of these three wise guys, we are told how God provided a bright, shining star in the sky to help them find their way. Again, we don't know the particulars, but we are lead to believe that this was one fat star that stood out from the rest and shone directly over the manger where Jesus was.

Now for several months, these wise guys followed this star that God had provided them, being that this was long before Rand McNally was born and good maps were hard to come by.

Keep in mind that God knew what He was doing. He specifically told these guys to follow the star and they should be okay. Being wise men, of course, they followed Gods instructions and being men, of course, they knew they would never need a map anyway.

Given this, I am constantly asking myself why these guys, whom I am told throughout this story are 'wise', had to drop by and ask Herod for directions?

I can almost see God smacking his forehead in frustration, 'The STAR, you idiots- follow the STAR!'

Here God put a huge arrow in their heavenly road map, and they had to go ask Herod for directions.

Not only that, but as soon as they leave Herods place, we are told AGAIN that they are greeted by a big, bright shining star that is shining over the manger!

I have never been accused of being especially bright, but I can tell you one thing. If God told me to take a present to a newborn Savior and He put a huge, bright shining star in the sky pointed on the shed and told me to follow it, I do believe I could find the Savior without Herods help. And I certainly wouldn't have taken any Myrrh for this Savior.

Besides, what kind of men were these guys? Everyone knows that a real man doesn't pull over and ask for directions.

Yes the story of the three wise men is a great part of the Christmas story. But maybe we shouldn't put too much emphasis on the wise part.

Our Great National Parks

I love those shows that have a lot of nature in it. I love shows that give you the top ten places to vacation. I love shows that explain all the wonderful adventures that this great planet has to offer us. I watch them often and will never apologize for that.

They had one on recently that gave us the top national parks to go visit. It was a great show. It had everything from the icy wilderness of Alaska to the everglade swamps of Florida. Every type of animal and environment was closely documented and explored.

I really enjoy stuff like that. Every time I watch these shows, I always make a mental note to myself that these are the places I want to go whenever the nickels 'n dimes and time permit. As a city boy, these nature parks really hold a sense of appeal to me. I can't imagine myself living in the wilderness, that's for sure, but I sure do love to watch these shows and would like to visit these places if I can.

I think shows like these teach us an important lesson. We as humans have come such a long way in our creative abilities.

We have created so many wonderful cities, buildings and monuments that clearly set us far and above the monkeys, lions, tigers and bears, oh my. Hey, you can argue that the Chimpanzee is a close cousin to me, but let me ask – has any Chimpanzee ever designed and built anything remotely close to the Empire State building? I don't think so.

But when you look at the national parks we have, you quickly realize that we humans are nowhere near what God has created for us. These parks have beauty, strength, balance and texture that we don't even come close to. The Empire State building is nice, certainly, but spend a day at the Teton National park and it doesn't take long to see that we are no threat to God's creativity.

That being said, I wanted to say something that just gets under my skin.

I like watching these shows about our national parks, but at the end of every show, I come away with the same feeling. Sure these parks are nice and I hope some day I can check them out for myself. But what a horrible feeling to know that they missed the one park that is most important to the fiber of all decent humans. The one national treasure that not only serves as a foundation to family values, but is well within reach of any American family no matter where they call home.

Of course, I'm talking about the baseball park.

Every spring, we humans come out of hibernation and take our children to the one park that has gapped generations to generations for generations. The baseball diamond is the one national park that we can all visit time and time again and experience the joy of celebrating our victories and agonizing our defeats. So many of life's lessons can be experienced at the ballpark.

We teach our children about persistence, it's not over until it's over, never give up and of course the margin between euphoric and humility are mere fractions.

At the baseball park, we learn that time is not the measure of success but getting the job done is.

At the baseball park, we learn that life isn't just about power and might, but more about finesse, strategy and determination.

At a baseball park, our children learn that you can't win every day, but it's important to try every day.

You don't always get a hit, but it's important to swing. You don't always make the catch, but it's important to pursue at all costs. You don't always have to look good, but you have to try and make the play.

Yes we have some wonderful national parks. I sure hope I live long enough to go check them out. But I have the greatest national park right here in Nashville. And I plan to go visit it as often as I can this summer.

When God made the heavens and the earth, it took Him six days. We are told that on the seventh day He rested. But I'm not stupid. There is no doubt that on the seventh day God went to the ballpark to catch a baseball game.

How do I know? Well I'm not scholar, but really ... the

Bible starts off with a baseball phrase after all... In the big inning .....

Just A Thought

Passport Of Life

One thing I am not is a world traveler. Not that I don't like to travel, mind you. I just haven't had that many opportunities to get out and about. When you live in my tax bracket, your biggest ambition is simply surviving from paycheck to paycheck.

With three teenage young ladies under my roof, I spend much of my time trying to create ideas into stories that will generate enough nickels and dimes to support their bustling lifestyles. I seldom get my head above the clouds of here and now to realize that there is an exciting world out there to explore.

I lived in San Diego for ions of calendar alterations and my travel log consisted of the stadium, beaches, wherever my paycheck beckoned, and a few forgettable trips south of the border that we won't get into here.

I moved to Nashville many Elvis sightings ago and have yet to venture far beyond the biscuit and gravy circuit.

I'd like to travel. There are many sights and sounds that I

would love to experience before my dance card of life runs out.

It has long been a dream of mine to spend some time in New York City. I'd love to spend a day at the stock exchange with someone who can tell me what all those frenzied people are actually doing. I want to go to a Broadway show, check out all those tall buildings, or drop by a few publisher's offices and see if I could recover a few manuscripts that I'm sure have collected enough dust by now.

I'd like to go to all the museums, monuments and sights of Washington, DC...drive through New England in October...play in every national park...ski the slopes of the Rockies...hula in Hawaii...go to a baseball game in every big league ball park.

I don't have much desire to travel overseas, though. For one thing, I'm basically a lazy guy. I have no desire to fumble through a dictionary for thirty minutes just to order a burger without mustard. It took me a lifetime to figure out what people were saying when I moved to the south. I'm sure not going to waste my time trying to figure out a completely new language and set of rules. So call me fickle, but I'll stay in America, thank you.

Another thing that keeps me from jumping over yonder is that it's just too old! Every time I watch a show that has scenes from Europe, they show buildings that were built long before nails, carpets or insulation were invented. Be it London, Paris, Athens, Rome or any other place, the buildings are always hundreds of years old. I mean, before we hit the next century, we should investigate to see if Europe has built anything new in this century! Call me young fashioned, but I just wouldn't feel comfortable going someplace that hasn't created anything new in the past several hundred years.

It's kind of sad, actually. The thought of traveling through this life without traveling through this world leaves me a little jetlag in the heart. San Diego and Nashville are great places, but I certainly hope that there is more to my life experiences than beaches and Opry's.

Then again, my travel log does show that I have been to swim meets, cross country meets, track meets, cheerleading camps, church camps, girl scouts, gymnastics, violin recitals, dance recitals, and various other major events that have kept me out of the mobile home circuit.

I guess when you really think about it, I have seen the best sights that the world has to offer, and I'm okay with that!

Just A Thought

Pulling The Lever

Pulling the lever.

It seems simple enough.

If you are a member of this family and have received at least 18 calendars from Insurance companies, you qualify to pull the lever.

If you are an engineer from MIT, or some guy who looks to the 'Far Side' comics for your wisdom ... you can pull the lever.

If your idea of a bad day is when your stocks drop 1/4 point, or when your food money has just been spent buying medicine for one of your children... you can still pull the lever.

They don't check the color of your skin ... they don't check your IQ ... they don't check your checking account ... they don't care what you wear, who you pray to or ask if you want smoking or non-smoking.

If you're a member of this family and have had at least 18 candles on your birthday cake, you can pull the lever.

Sometimes it almost seems silly. You go to the designated

location, sign their book, walk through a curtain, and in a most private, uneventful manner, you pull the lever. No one claps for you when you step out from the curtain. There are no bands playing, celebrating your efforts. No fireworks. No confetti. No pomp or circumstances. You just quietly walk out with a sigh of satisfaction for having done your part for the family.

It's called voting.

A rather simple act that represents so much of what makes this the greatest country in this ever-changing world we live in. Most people in the world never get a chance to pull the lever. So many people in the world go through their life without ever having any say in what goes on in the world they live in.

But we do.

Every other year we get to go behind the curtain and pull the lever.

And for over two hundred years, there have always been the same two candidates for us to choose between.

Choice #1 – Stay the course

Choice #2 – Let's change directions.

Certainly the names and faces have changed over the years, but every time we step behind the curtain, our choice is always the same... do we want to stay the course or change directions? Everybody has an equal voice in the matter. Everybody gets to pull the lever one time.

Whether they burn the flag, belong to the KKK, a preppie

country club, or a conservative, right-wing church. Each person gets to pull the lever one time.

An equal voice no matter where you stand on life's ladder.

It's a pretty good system that was created for us by our forefathers. It's certainly not a perfect system by any stretch, but it's clearly the best system devised for a government 'by the people'… if we all do our part … if we all use our voice … if we all pull the lever just once.

It's a simple act that doesn't come with a lot of pomp or circumstance. However, when we pull the lever, we are telling the whole world that our voice is a voice to be heard.

Just A Thought

Knowing What Matters

A young man recently asked me what the advantage was of being an old man. I had three days to think about this question while my lawyer worked to get me out of jail – something about smacking a guy upside the head with a two-by-four is wrong, they tell me.

Though I vehemently insist on referring to my age as 21 with 34 years of experience, I suppose I am able to shed some knowledge on this thing called the aging process.

So being a giving guy – who also has a mounting legal bill to pay – I have decided to share with you some random thoughts about the advantage of getting older.

Credit reports – doesn't matter

Paying bills on time – doesn't matter

Owning a home – doesn't matter

Having the latest SUV – doesn't matter

Having a drink with your daughter every week – matters

Wearing the latest styles – doesn't matter

Taking a cruise – doesn't matter

Having shiny white teeth – doesn't matter

Keeping up with the trends – doesn't matter
Going camping with your friends – matters
Having gray hair – doesn't matter
Having no hair – doesn't matter
That extra flab that won't go away – doesn't matter
Feeling two steps behind everyone else – doesn't matter
Knowing you can't party like you use to – doesn't matter
Looking in the mirror and being able to smile – matters
Achieving that dream in your heart – doesn't matter
Finding the love of your life – doesn't matter
Solving all the world's problems – doesn't matter
Making a difference – doesn't matter
Trying – matters
Going to the right church – doesn't matter
Memorizing scriptures – doesn't matter
Following all of life's rules – doesn't matter
Knowing right from wrong – doesn't matter
Seeing God as a friend you can trust – matters

I have no idea if I'm going to be very good at this senior citizen stuff. I wasn't much of an adult. Actually, I was a pretty good teenager and have pretty much stayed there in my heart through the years.

It's not that I ignored the doesn't matter items on my list. Actually, I've done okay in most of them, I suppose. To be honest, I really don't have a problem in pursuing those things.

To me it's more an issue of understanding those items in our life that do matter and making sure that you do take advantage of them whenever you can. It's a wonderful peace you have when you get to the down slope of your life knowing that although you may have screwed up many things, you have done well with those things that mattered.

I have not made a lot of money. I have not been very good in business. I have not garnered many of life's toys and pleasures. I have not been able to reach my dreams.

But I have also not made any enemies. Well, with the exception of the young man recovering from the two-by-four I planted on his sideburns. But frankly, he had it coming to him.

As you get older, you tend to reflect more on your past. When you do, you find most of your thoughts deal with relationships. I assure you it will matter if those thoughts bring a smile or a sigh of missed opportunity.

Just a Thought

Life's Measuring Stick

Being a creative guy who spends a lot of time thinking –
okay, some of you snicker and say daydreaming might be a
better choice of words here, but stay with me – I have come
up with the one word that would be the ultimate measuring
stick for everyone who takes a stroll though this wonderful
thing we call life.

It's just one word, but in such a diverse world as ours, it's
the only word that we can use fairly to measure the quality of
ones life on this planet. If you apply this one word to every
human being regardless of the resume of life they bring with
them, you can always make a fair assessment of their life. In
fact, if each of us used this one word in every decision we
make throughout the day, it would have an absolute impact
on the direction our lives go.

Some of you are thinking I am going to talk about love
today, but you would be wrong. Not even close. I've seen
pictures of mothers holding their starving child in African
villages. I've seen the deep love in their eyes. There simply is
no way you can use love to measure the quality of ones life.

There are many who have a lot of love but little quality in their lives. Love is not the answer.

And don't even think for a minute that the word is money. PLEASE. How many examples do we need of people who make more money than they'll ever need yet live a life that conjures up the word pathetic much more than quality. Money is fun if you can get it, but it really has little to do with measuring the quality of your life.

The word I'm thinking about is OPPORTUNITY.

With just this one word, you can measure the quality of every person's life.

With just this one word, you can fairly assess the quality of anyone's life, regardless of the resume they carry with them.

I've heard young people ask how God could judge people when we live in such a diverse world that really isn't all that fair. The simple answer is opportunity. I'm certain that God would look at that woman holding her child in that village in Africa and understand that she has had so few opportunities to better her life compared to those who live in much better situations. I can look at my own life and see how opportunities have influenced the quality of my life, both in the good ways and the bad. I can see some failures in my life and refuse to beat myself up because I can see that given the opportunities I had at the time, I did about as good as I could expect to.

I can also see some failures in my life and wince as if biting into a lemon as I realize that my failure was the result of me missing the opportunity that was right in front of me.

The opportunities in my life – whether they were seized or missed – can make a fair judgment of the quality of my life.

The thing about opportunity is that they intertwine with everybody else. I've had some failures that I can honestly look at and see that the failure was not because I failed to seize the opportunity, but because there was someone else who was in a position and had the opportunity to make a difference, but didn't for whatever reason.

Certainly, how I handled the opportunities in my life has had an impact on the opportunities my daughters faced.

Every day we all face opportunities that will affect not only the quality of our lives, but of the lives of those around us.

And they grow. Every opportunity you seize creates even more opportunities.

Certainly, the richest man in the world does not necessarily have a quality life, he just has more opportunities and the quality of his life depends on how he handles those opportunities. He can use his wealth as an opportunity to help that lady in the African village by creating opportunities for her, or he can sit around and think of ways he can create even more wealth for himself.

Gotta Go … my daughter just called and I have an opportunity to go meet her for lunch – which will make me a wealthy man today, indeed.

It's all about opportunities.

Just A Thought

Lights, Camera, Christmas

There's something missing, here. I mean, it's Christmas and I know that something is just not right...I can feel it.

Let's see...we have our Christmas tree up. I'm the only one in the family who still insists on a 'real' Christmas tree. Call me old fashioned but I refuse to commercialize my life with a perfectly plastic, fold up Christmas tree. Of course I do worry that I am going to have to get bigger trees each year as we always buy new 'special' ornaments each year to add to our already bulging collection. And of course, to suggest that we throw out some of the old ones... you know, the ones that you can't even read anymore, have seen most of its paint chip away, and serve only as conversation pieces at parties... is like asking a teenager to put some order into the war zone under their bed. It will never happen.

But for now, the Christmas tree is up... that is not the part of Christmas that I am missing.

We have all our decorations up.

The outdoor lights are up. Each year I keep promising to do something different with the lights, and each year, after wrestling with the lights for hours, I always end up doing the same thing with them. I think there is a name for that, but I won't get into that now.

We have all the Christmas nic-nacs out and about the house to transform our humble abode into a Christmas fantasy land.

We've been shopping and have maintained our tradition of spending more than we promised ourselves we would.

No, as I look about our house and checkbook, I can see that Christmas is truly here and in full swing.

So what could be missing from all of this?

As I sit down and browse through our TV listings, I realize that what is missing from the Christmas celebration is Christmas specials on the TV.

Oh sure, they still run those cartoon specials that we all love year after year...Charlie Brown... the Grinch and my all-time favorite – Mr. Mago's Christmas Carol... But I'm talking about those Christmas specials that we all looked forward to each year when I was growing up.

Andy Williams, Dean Martin, Carol Burnette, Danny Kaye, Red Skelton, Perry Como and the others.

They all had regular variety shows and each year at Christmas, they would put their best foot forward with a holiday show that would really ignite the spirit of the season in each of us. It seemed like every night there was a festive holiday special of winter wonderful celebration that the whole family could enjoy. These specials, surrounded by the animated holiday stories that we loved, seemed to capture the spirit of the season and create in all of us a since of excited anticipation as we waited for the morning of all mornings to arrive.

But today they seem to have lost the ability to create that Christmas spirit through our televisions. Variety shows have been replaced by sitcoms and drama series that are merely clones unto themselves. Sure, most of these shows have their Christmas episodes, but the story lines tend to be overused, predictable and pretty much the same from show to show and channel to channel.

Remember how Andy Williams had his whole family join him for his Christmas show?

Danny Kaye always had a lot of children on his show.

Red Skelton and Carol Bumette had those great skits.

Dean Martin and Perry Como had such great holiday music.

And there were always a few specials involving the flavor of the day hottest artist at the time that would bring along some of his or her friends.

It was a lot of holiday music, laughter and variety that helped us keep the spirit of the season alive each day. And of course, It wasn't Christmas without the Bob Hope special from some war zone.

Nowadays, you get those same animated specials, and a flood of manufactured episodic sleepers.

Somehow Christmas doesn't seem to be the same without those TV specials of the past. Christmas specials aren't special anymore. There are no shows with those who have been in our living room all year long giving back a little something special. Few Christmas songs being sung by the fire...no Christmas skits that tickle our lighter side... no jingle bells and sleigh rides with our favorite celebrities.

My kids don't know what I'm talking about, and that's too bad.

I guess that's why VCRs were invented. We just can't depend on the networks to keep the Christmas spirit alive for us anymore.

Just A Thought

Magoo Made Me Do It

I'm a guy who comes from that 'other' generation. You know the peace, love and hippies kinda guy. I still remember when Time magazine came out with a picture of a computer on the cover and the title read, "Someday they'll be in every home". Of course, the nerds said, "Far out!" while us cool surfer dudes said something to the effect that those people down at Time magazine were smoking some weird stuff.

Since then, many of us flower-powered people have reluctantly accepted this new mechanical monster into our lives. Certainly we are no match to the younger generation who grew up on computers and have mastered the fine art of point-and-clickology. Most of us shy away from getting too connected to the information highway.

It's a trust issue that keeps telling us that this computer stuff is too good to be true and we know that somewhere out there in cyberspace big brother is messing with us and we aren't going to have nothin' to do with that!

But when you want something bad enough, you tend to

put those paranoia thoughts aside and take the plunge into this new world of techno-surfing.

Actually it was Mr Magoo's fault.

Since the beginning of time, I have been a huge fan of Mr Magoo's Christmas Carol. The music is great and it's a wonderful way of bringing Dickens immortal Christmas classic to such a delightful level as to make us think that Charles Dickens in fact wrote it with Mr Magoo specifically in mind. It's one Christmas show I watch several times a year, especially during those dog days of heat and humidity when I need a cool down.

I mentioned to some of my buddies that I couldn't find a good copy of this classic and was frustrated having to watch a copy I recorded off my TV about 15 years ago. The copy I made was awful with cut off scenes and several TV commercials of products that no longer exist.

Someone mentioned that I should go on eBay and see if they have any and bid for a copy. He said it so matter-of-factly and made it sound like it was no big deal. Of course I pretty much blew him off. I'm not about to jump into that people-waiting-to-rip-you-off web site.

Young people think they're so smart.

I got home that night and quietly found my way into this eBay site. Nervously clicking and scrolling my way through the mega-mounds of useless products until I finally found what I was looking for.

There it was – four copies of Mr Magoo's Christmas Carol waiting for me to stake a claim.

I followed all the steps and before I knew it, the moment of truth was upon me.

Should I go for it and make a bid?

How can I trust this tape to be the real deal?

How do I know that eBay isn't just another government conspiracy that stands for the Easy Bilking Agency for America's Youth?

I took the plunge. After all, it's not like it was some useless item I really didn't need. This was Mr Magoo's Christmas Carol, for crying out loud. Certainly worth taking a little risk to obtain, you would think.

I made my bid.

Sunday the bidding got to the highest bid I agreed to and there was still well over a day of bidding left to go. I thought I was toast and began to brush this whole experience off as another scam I wasn't going to get caught up in.

Monday night we were down to the final hour and my bid was still holding up.

I was a neurotic mess.

I was certain that there were thousands of cyber-monsters out there just waiting for the final minutes to jump in and snag my Magoo out of my clutches.

My male ego kicked in and I found myself talking tough-guy to my computer.

"Common, bring it on! Just try to out bid me, mister! You're messin' with the wrong guy, ya know! I ain't no fool buster, I'm the ultimate Magoo fan! Don't EVEN think you can out bid me on this one, pal!"

I was pacing around the house, snorting and sucking my chest in, bobbing my head around like a tough guy ready to take anyone on.

I even spit on my carpet.

I settled into my seat ready to win.

30 seconds … refresh …

20 seconds … refresh …

10 seconds … refresh …

1 second … refresh …

"bidding over"

I sat there with a glazed look staring at my computer.

No one else bid.

Mr Magoo was mine.

Mr Tough Guy celebrated, dancing around the house, high-fiving my walls, refrigerator and ceiling, making macho grunts of victory and generally behaving in a manner that made me appreciate the fact that I live alone.

I emailed the seller and arraigned to pay so I could receive my trophy.

Four days later, I was sitting in my home watching a wonderful copy of Mr Magoo's Christmas Carol – with no commercials – and tears rolling down my cheeks. Tears that reflected not only the joy in finally having a copy of this story I have loved for so long, but tears that came from the satisfaction of knowing that this is one flower-powered hippie that is willing to take a chance and jump into a new generation of cyber toys, gadgets and ecommerce – but only for something worthwhile.

Will I do it again?

Probably not.

I think standing in the delivery room waiting for my daughter to arrive was a more calming event than waiting on big brother out there to try and out bid me for Mr Magoo.

Besides…. and I am NOT making this up …. I was at a department store the other day and saw the very same copy of Magoo's Christmas Carol on a rack – 3 copies, no less – for $7 each.

Don't ask me how much I paid on eBay.

Suffice it to say that had I gone shopping at said department store that evening instead of trying to figure out this trendy new world of cyber shopping, I could have easily been sitting here with three good copies of Magoo.

I believe my cyber shopping days are over, folks!

Just A Thought

I Stand Alone

I'm going to say it. I know there will be many who will disagree with me. Some may be outraged at what I am saying – but they will only confirm that they didn't get my point. But call me what you will, I feel strongly that somebody has to say this.

There is a trend going about that has me troubled. I understand it and so I bite my tongue and say nothing because if I said what I feel, I know I would be the receiver of great wrath of those who hear me. But last night reflected exactly what I am feeling and so I will share it with you.

I was at a hockey game last night and during a break, they introduced a young man from college who has started his own non-profit organization to help the people in Haiti, raised over 10 thousand dollars and created a 5K run to benefit the struggling people of Haiti – while going to school. Pretty impressive and the sold out crowd gave the young man a polite round of appreciation.

About a half hour later they introduced a young man who is an officer in the military who just got back from Iraq. This man received an impressive standing ovation that truly was heartwarming even for me.

My problem is not so much the reaction to the military person. I understand we live in a society that puts great value in anyone who fights our battles for freedom. I get that. But what troubles me is that this officer received an impressive standing ovation and for all we know he could have worked in a warehouse in Bagdad and never saw any action but that didn't matter to us – he's an all-American hero.

Meanwhile it took a few minutes to tell us all the work this young college kid is doing to help those struggling neighbors in Haiti and we stayed in our seats and politely applauded.

I believe one of the worst effects of 9/11 is that we have become a testosterone nation. I understand it as I have become a part of it as well. But I will go out on a limb here and say that this testosterone mentality we have created will absolutely make us weaker, not stronger. You only need to look at Washington DC to understand this. Be it the 'right' or the 'left', this macho testosterone mentality has created a dig-in approach that we will never compromise as we are bigger and we are stronger and we are tougher! We will never get anything done because we have lost our ability to be compassionate.

We have lost our ability to care for one another. Those are signs of weakness and by God we will never compromise our toughness.

Some would yell at me and state that I am being disrespectful of our military ... it's because of them that I have the freedom to say what I am saying ... and thank God there aren't many like me or our country would never be free!

Go ahead and give me your best shot. I understand the consequences of 9/11 we live with.

But suppose this young man saw what I saw last night. Suppose he thought as I did ... gee, I work so hard to raise a little money to help those struggling in Haiti and the rewards are token at best. I could join the military and wear my uniform to a hockey game and get a rousing standing ovation regardless of what I've done... So he joins the military, goes to war and gets killed in action, comes home in a box and they put a nice statue up in his home town. The good news is that he dies a hero. The bad news is that there are no heroes left helping those struggling people in Haiti, Africa, South America or in our own back yard.

And with that, I have to ask how many of the thousands of young people we have lost in war also had the heart and compassion to have contributed to those struggling in Haiti, Africa, South America and in our own back yard?

When God created Adam, we are told that he stepped back and realized that Adam needed a partner, so he created Eve. Is it merely a coincident that the main ingredient missing in Eve from Adam is the testosterone gene?

God understood that man can not live by testosterone alone... we need compassion... we need to care ... we need to be loving enough to compromise.

Then and only then will we be strong.

God got it right… after all it is noted that Eve was the last thing God created in the creation story.

We need to understand as well that this testosterone mentality we embrace will continue to make us weaker unless we compliment it with a strong dose of compassion, caring and compromise.

It needed to be said.

Just A Thought

I'm All Heart

Two things happened to me recently that gave me much room to pause and reevaluate this thing we call life.

The first incident came when a publisher asked me to email her a head shot to run with a story of mine she wanted to use. Though it's been a while, this is no big deal and I always have my 8X10, B&W head shot ready for just this occasion. So I pull it up to make sure it's the right one when something blatantly distressing occurs to me.

This picture, though quite artistic and debonair, is a good twenty years old.

If you're between twenty and forty years old, that's no big deal, but when you're between thirty five and fifty five, that's flat out delusional.

Since I am a firm believer that misleading is reserved only for politicians and used car salesmen, I scrambled to find a more current representation of my head to send along. With a tearful sniffle I send my mug shot to the publisher, knowing that I have done the right thing, but also keenly aware that

I have just reduced a pile of snazzy 8X10s to ancient history status.

I have become a 'has-been'.

About the same time, I went to have my yearly physical, which after fifty brings back memories of that first old car you had that required a constant, nagging duct tape mechanics just to keep the damn thing running for another thousand miles. It was determined by the doc that it would be a good idea for me to have a thing called a Cardiac Scoring test. For the medically lame like me, this is merely a cat scan of my heart to see if the plumbing is still in shape. At fifty five it becomes more a medical process of elimination, and what with so many of your parts being eliminated as to their usefulness, it's a good idea to make sure the old ticker and arteries do not require any duct tape.

So I had the rather simple and yet quite expensive test done and waited for the nurse to report back to me, praying that my inbox would not be inundated with advertisements from mortuaries. When I finally got the call from the nurse, she reported that my heart was, and I quote, 'Youthful'. At fifty five I am at minimal risk of anything going wrong with the old ticker and my arteries are as clear as a teenagers.

So the doc and I can move forward with the duct tape mechanics of getting older knowing that the main engine is in great shape and poised to take this old man many more miles down the road of life.

It occurred to me as I was driving home the other day that aging can be a funny lesson in contradictions. For many, your attitude is the last thing to grow old – at least you hope so.

The problem with me being over fifty is that in my heart, I am still wrestling with the issue of what I want to be when I grow up. And the problem with this is that the answer has remained the same for years – why would I want to grow up? I never asked to be an adult and now that I'm moving into senior citizenship, I sure as hell have no desire to go down that road either.

I'd rather look at myself as a twenty year old with thirty five years of experience.

As my three daughters can attest to, I have always been a strong proponent that people should listen to and follow their heart. How many times have my daughters called me for advice and heard me say the same thing; 'I'll give you my opinion as long as you promise me that the last voice you listen to is your heart.'

I see way too many people who have lost this art of listening to and following their hearts. How sad it is to see people living their lives by what others are saying or doing instead of trusting their hearts to lead them.

Yes I am getting older and I guess I'll have to upgrade my collection of 8X10, B&Ws to present my readers with a more representative exterior of who it is telling these stories. I'd prefer the younger shots of course, but I'm running out of duct tape.

I take comfort in knowing that this is one guy who has documentation now that I am a man who follows his own words. With so many other parts showing the signs of getting older, my heart is about the only thing I have left that remains youthful and rebellious against the aging process.

I will gleefully continue to listen to and follow my heart, thank you.

Just A Thought

Fatherhood Flops

It's just not fair.

Someone told me recently that men make lousy fathers. Well excuse me, but if you really want to be honest about it, men have never been good father material. They were not raised to be good fathers.

From the moment they are born, females are being prepared for motherhood. Their first toy is almost always a cute little doll. And in this wonderful world of modern technology, they have created dolls that will give a little girl first hand experience with every aspect of child rearing. She will learn how to change diapers, handle feedings, burping, tantrums, bathing, fixing hair, kissing owies, and many other tasks that will come in handy many years down the road when the dolls become the real thing.

Females are well prepared for motherhood. It's no wonder that a young man, who has spent many years playing catch with his Dad in the back yard, will smile at the camera during a national telecast and say, "Hi Mom!"

Females play mother all through their childhood. By the

time they get married and begin the process of splitting chromosomes, they have had many years of practice. Females make great mothers, no doubt about it.

But what about Dad?

He spent his childhood crashing cars, bulldozing the back yard with trucks and tractors, saving the world with an assortment of inter-galactic weaponry and learning the fine art of turning a single into a double.

By the time a boy becomes a man and earns the privilege of passing out cigars, he is no more prepared for fatherhood than Hitler would be for Passover.

Com'on, let's lighten up on fatherhood already.

I think most of us do a pretty good job considering we haven't had much training for the job. Men may not be able to hold a stick to women when it comes to parenting, but we certainly do much better than we are given credit for.

Would you condemn a woman for not being able to fix her car if she had absolutely no training in auto mechanics?

Of course you wouldn't.

Would you condemn a woman for not being able to hit to the opposite field and advance the runner to third, when she had a childhood that told her that girls should not be found on a baseball field?

Of course not!

Sure there is a lot of room for improvement, but let's be fair to the men of the world. How good would you be if you were hired for a job you had no training for?

Raising children is the most demanding, toughest job that

we will ever take on in our lives. Men are certainly handicapped from the time they begin to pass out those cigars, but they are not hopeless.

Fatherhood is easily the greatest challenge a man will face in his lifetime. How sad it is that it will also be one of the few challenges he faces with so little preparation for. He is raised in a macho world of rough, tough, tumbling toys and then thrown into a world of gentleness, compassion and patience.

It's a wonder that men get as far as they do, if you ask me.

There are many men who take a lot of pride in their roles as fathers. Yes there are far too many men out there that do more harm than good. But those of us who are trying, feel bad about these cases too, and become frustrated with the image that has been built against us.

Most of us are really trying. We may fumble a lot through diaper duty, mess up our feeding assignments and create a number of blunders in our efforts to become good dads, but in all fairness, I think we do a pretty good job.

You simply don't learn much about fatherhood when you grow up playing with Tonka Trucks.

For most men, the "light" goes on when the doctor puts that bundle of broken chromosomes in your arms in the delivery room. At that moment, a man becomes a Dad, and most of us understand from that moment on, that the priorities of their world has just changed forever.

We're not as good as Moms, but a lot of us understand the priorities.

Just A Thought

Fix It

There is a lot of debate these days about the Health Care in this great country. The politicians will tell us this debate is, well, HEALTHY and a part of what makes our country so great. That's all well and good I suppose, as long as somewhere in this debate the politicians actually listen. Being older and wiser of course, I'm going to do my civic duty by sharing with our fine people that we send to Washington a simple, easy to understand explanation with no attempt at being politically correct.

So listen up, Politicians!

[DEEP BREATH]

Every evening I come home and turn on the evening news which is surrounded by very expensive, elaborate commercials by pharmaceutical companies pushing pills I can't run to the store to buy, but have to ask my doctor about, but when I do he says nothing because he prescribes my medications brought to him via a nice paycheck by the very same pharmaceutical company that brought me those expensive, elaborate TV commercials, which makes me wonder why they spend so much on TV commercials if they are also spending money pushing their pills with my doctor, but I'm told this is not so, because these poor pharmaceutical companies actually have to charge so much for their little pills because research is so expensive, which makes me wonder why don't they stop spending money on their expensive, elaborate TV commercials that they apparently don't need because they already purchased my doctor and put that money into research, but again I'm told that I just don't understand, which I don't and is why I asked the question in the first place, because I don't understand when I get a medical bill and read that my simple 'procedure' that only took about 30 minutes cost $17,000.00 and when I look at the very small print I see that the little bandage I now own on my side cost $87.43 which strikes me as odd because I'm thinking that I saw the same box of bandages at Wal Mart for like $2.00 and I'm asking myself what is so special about this bandage that keeps the doctor from picking up the same thing at Wal Mart, but again I'm told I just don't understand, which I don't, and that is why I asked the question, because I am told that I should trust my doctor, which I do, but I have a problem understanding how any of this medical financing makes any sense, which it never will, so we go to our polls and vote for our neighbors to go Washington and try to make sense of all this medical chaos because we all want to be able to have good health care, but then we find out that those same pharmaceutical companies that bring us those elaborate, expensive TV commercials also bring us those constant, elaborate, expensive campaign commercials because, well, if you want to win an election, who better to do your TV commercials than those pharmaceutical companies that are experts at spending money on TV commercials that we apparently don't need because they also spend a lot of money on making sure doctors only give patients their pills and tell us they need to charge us a fortune for these pills because of research, and well, what politician wouldn't want that kind of company working for their campaign after all, so when the debate about health care comes up, the politicians are careful to avoid the real issues because, well, they're going to need some more fancy commercials in a few years when they run for re election and they don't want to bite the hand that feeds them after all, so they cleverly make the debate whether the government should control health care or not, which frankly has most of us scratching our heads trying to figure out how we got to this point. [Exhale]

If we learned anything from Richard Nixon it is that if you really want to find the truth, you have to follow the money.

We want a strong military, but we don't want our taxes to be spent on $200.00 toilet seats and $300.00 hammers ... we want good health care, but we don't want our health insurance companies to have to spend $87.43 on a band aide ... we want politicians who represent the good of the people, not the good of the companies that bring us expensive, elaborate re election TV commercials that we don't really need.

Yes, we have a serious problem with obesity in our country. But the issue is not simply fat people, as much as it's fat wallets.

It's called GREED – fix THAT Mr Politician!

Just A Thought

God and Dad

Someone asked me once what the best lesson I ever learned from being a Dad. But before I answer that, let me say something about my girls.

I have three daughters who are now grown up and out of the nest. It has always been my pleasure – and honor – to call them my girls. It still is. I suspect that I have caused them a lot more grief and embarrassment than they have me.

They were not perfect children, but they were not raised to be.

I don't think any of them will be on the cover of Time magazine, but I am certain that they will not be on the Post Office wall, either.

Everybody who knows my girls loves them. They have few, if any, enemies. They are simply good people who work hard and are very considerate towards those around them.

As their Dad, my love for my girls is thorough and without blemish. There is no scenario that would ever make any one of my daughters not welcome in my home. I can think of no situation where I would ever turn my back on my girls.

There is nothing they could ever do to make me stop loving them.

I have never wanted my girls to fear me. I wanted them to know that they can always come to me with whatever is on their heart and know that I will not judge, but listen. I may not be able to solve their problems, but at least I can always present to them the options for what they face. '

There have been many times when they have gone through some tough times where I have been frustrated because they didn't come to me for comfort, advice or simply a shoulder to cry on. But I also take pride in their ability to work through those difficult times and appreciate their confidence in being able to solve their own problems.

I have never taken pleasure in seeing them learn their lessons the hard way. I have always encouraged them to think and try to learn the lessons of life without having to go through any valleys.

I celebrate their successes for as long as I can and move quickly to forgive and get past any bad times.

So when asked what important lessons I have learned from being a Dad, my answer is simple.

If a regular guy like me has this kind of love for his children, then how much more must God have for His children?

We have a pretty sad perception of God I think. So many people live in fear that if they don't walk the perfect path, God will be ready to punish them and punish them hard. I cringe when I hear people say that God took them through some horrible valley in life so that they would learn a lesson. And it breaks my heart to hear people say that God does not listen or answer prayers.

Being a Dad has made my spiritual walk a much more rewarding and profound celebration of God.

There is nothing special about me. I am simply a guy who has done a good job of being a Dad to three young ladies.

God is love defined.

God's love for us is so much greater than we can comprehend. He doesn't want us to fear Him. He doesn't want to take us through valleys in order to teach us a lesson. He doesn't want us to feel He is unapproachable or that He doesn't hear our voice. And I am bewildered at people constantly praying for Gods will in their life. Gods will for us has always been the same. He wants us to be happy and at peace with ourselves and those around us.

I know that my love for my daughters is special and without blemish. It is such a joy to know that everything I have said about my daughters, God has said about me ten fold.

Now that's some powerful love.

Just A Thought

Dude, Just Tennis Shoes, Okay

Well I just had one of the worst experiences of my life. I just got home from buying a pair of shoes.

It started off easy enough. I got a check in the mail from an editor who actually paid me for one of my stories. As I often do with surprise money like that, I decided I would splurge a little and buy something just for me.

I really needed a pair of tennis shoes, so I headed off to the mall to pamper my feet.

Let me start by saying I am 100% male when it comes to shopping. I don't like it. I like to go into a store, grab some proximity of what I'm in need of, pay for it and head out the door.

I'm a no frills shopper.

Browsing has no place in my vocabulary.

And I especially detest walking into a store and being greeted by a bunch of commission-hungry salespeople. I almost never buy anything at those stores.

So here I am walking into the mall with an excellent game plan. 15 minutes to grab a pair of tennis shoes, 30 minutes to browse through my favorite book store, and another 30 minutes at the food garden packing away the sinful dogs with mayo, mustard, relish and plenty of onions.

I slip into the first sporting store thinking that they might have just what I need, being that their walls were decked with a various array of tennis shoes.

As I walked in, this kid who looked like an NBA ref a few years shy of puberty greets me with a perky smile and, "Can I help you, sir?"

I quickly brush the kid off with a confident " Naw, I just need to pick up a pair of tennis shoes."

"Great" says the perky punkster, not realizing that he is wasting his energy on a guy with little appetite for salesmanship.

"What kind do you need?"

Rule number one when shopping is that you never let a salesperson know that you have no idea of what you are looking for, or what he is talking about.

"White" I say… he laughs.

"Well what do you do?" he inquires.

I pause "I'm a writer"

He laughs again.

"No, what do you need the shoes for?" he smiles.

I pause "My feet?"

He laughs.

"That's funny… I mean what do you need them for… basketball?… racquetball?… aerobics?… tennis?… jogging?…"

I smile with painful hesitation, "Walking?"

"Oh, so you're a walker? So how long you been walking, mister?"

"Well," I say through my grinding teeth, "From what I've been told, since I was around nine months old."

He laughs out loud... I'm ready to hit the bookstore.

"Well you're in luck today because all the walking shoes over there with the red tag are on special for ya!"

Well I'm about ready to skip the shoes and head straight for the super dog as I fumble through the walking shoes looking for a red tag. I mention to the young lad that they all seem awfully heavy and ask if he has just a plain pair of white tennis shoes?

"Well sir, those give you great support and are a great buy this week at only $85.00!"

Which was the last thing I heard before "Someone call 911!"

We seem to have lost touch with the simple things in life. Why can't someone walk into a store and buy a simple pair of shoes for just kicking around the house? Why does a pair of tennis shoes have to come with so much technological advancement that instead of comfort, you feel like your walking around in cinder blocks? I MIGHT spend $85 bucks for a pair of shoes to go with my tux if they ever invite me to the Grammy Awards. But I will NEVER pay $85 bucks for a pair of tennis shoes to get me from my computer to the couch.

So I bought a book for 20 bucks, thinking I could curl up on the couch and read all the wonderful stories barefoot.

Somebody stop the madness!

Just A Thought

Emotionally Scientific

I have said it many times before that when it comes to awkward comedy, there is nothing better than watching a room full of scientists during a big event.

For the record, I am not mocking science or making fun of the fine people who brought us Tang and microwave ovens. I am the first to salute the men and women who are leading the way in our world of advancement towards the new frontiers. God knows that if everyone thought like me, the wonderful world of Chimpanzees would be horrified at any conversation putting them in close proximity to the human race.

But for a simple minded fellow like myself, I don't think you can find better entertainment than watching scientists react to another probe making a safe landing on Mars, or explaining with so much enthusiasm how they have studied for months a star far, far away and the little blip of light variance has caused them to determine that there is an Earth like planet going around this star!

Scientists just don't do emotions.

They are too busy studying books and becoming smart people to have any idea of proper technique for high-fives, fist pumps and certainly the art of hugging another human. They are not very smooth at handling giddy moments, that's for sure. I just can't get enough of these awkward moments of giddy scientists.

I mention this because last week, we had an event in my area that truly was a cool moment to witness. A full eclipse of the Sun is something you want to experience.

My city was smack in the middle of the path of totality, so my daughter and I didn't have to wrestle with the crowds and traffic as we knew the perfect place near our neighborhood to take this natural phenomena in. Being that the total eclipse was scheduled for 1:58pm in our area, we packed a nice picnic and of course an ample supply of mimosa makings and staked out our chairs and specialty glasses to wait for the big event.

We were not disappointed.

Watching the Moon slowly move in front of the Sun created a great atmosphere of anticipation for that one moment of totality. For two minutes, the afternoon became night. You could turn in every direction and see a beautiful Sunrise. It was a remarkable experience that I felt so lucky to have been a part of.

That evening, there were many reports throughout the country about this total eclipse that I had witnessed with my daughter and mimosas. Most of the reports showed scientists sitting at tables on mountain tops or desolate, remote areas with monitors, cameras and gadgets that will entertain and enlighten them with data for months to come.

When the Sun reappeared, there was another great show of awkward emotions and comments from giddy scientists on how all the data they have obtained will be so important for the advancement of mankind.

For me, I kind of felt sorry for the scientists. They spent so much time and energy explaining all the math and science for why this happened. They will spend so much time in the coming months devouring all this data in order to take us a step further in explaining our universe.

But somehow I feel like they miss the point.

For me, the lesson is watching a small, insignificant ball of rocks that has no real purpose in our universe other than serving as a night-light for our planet, taking on the much larger, more significant ball of fire that is so important to our existence and for two minutes in the middle of the day, turn off the lights.

When the odds are against you or you feel insignificant, there's your inspiration!

I think it's important to pay attention and appreciate the many examples God gives us in nature that can go a long way in building our faith in God as well as ourselves. A small insignificant ant with apparently no muscle structure can easily carry ten times it's weight like it is foam, yet the powerful, muscle packed gorilla can not.

Trees can go through brilliant, colorful seasons of death in the Fall, only to come back in beautiful splendor of life every Spring.

The more we pay attention to and appreciate all that nature shows us, the more confidence we have in our own ability to achieve great things in our life.

But for pure entertainment, you gotta love those giddy scientists.

Just A Thought

A Sunny Paycheck

As a starving writer, I'm always looking over the job market to see if there might be better job opportunities that would satisfy my friendly bill collectors as well as my need not to work hard so I can spend more time just writing.

I automatically rule out any blue-collar jobs. They work too hard, get paid too little and are often not appreciated enough for their efforts.

I don't want to be a supervisor anywhere. They don't have to work too hard, but they do have to put up with the many complaints of those they supervise. I'm afraid I would agree with them too often and end up losing my job.

I could never be a businessman. The thought of sitting behind a desk in a three-piece suit listening to elevator music from 8-5 every day gives this free spirit the willies. I'm just not cut out to be a company guy.

I'm a lousy salesman, which probably accounts for the well-deserved title of 'starving writer'. I'm too honest and opinionated to be much good for selling stuff.

But I did find a job that would be ideal. A job that is highly respected within the community. A job that pays well and provides a moderate level of celebrity. Most importantly, it permits a high level of mistakes without any consequences, and you can perform your job from any location you want.

I'm thinking about being a weatherman.

How many of you work at a job where you can be totally wrong one day, yet warmly welcomed back the next? A weatherman calls for snow, we all gather at the store for our milk, bread and beer on our way home from work, only to wake up the next morning with a sunny mother nature laughing at our sorry soft selves. We grumble on our way to work, swearing that the weatherman gets kickbacks from the grocery stores. Yet that evening, we will be glued once again to our television to see what the weatherman has to say about tomorrow.

It's a no-lose situation.

There are no consequences for being wrong because the weatherman spends a lot of time convincing us that mother nature is very fickle and how we happen to live on some fence, where pending storms can go either way. They get paid well whether the weather is right or wrong.

And we all warmly wave at them as they serve as grand marshals in our community parades.

What a great job!

Besides, I wouldn't need all that computer stuff to predict the weather. I have a bum elbow that flares up every time there's a change in the weather. I'm sure everyone has a relative with a unique, sure-fire way of predicting the weather.

Drop me a note and tell me about it. I might just start my own weather service. I've never been in a parade, and this just might be my ticket.

Just A Thought

An Alarming Thought

History has always been an intriguing subject for me. In my many years of lower learning, history has always been the one subject I knew I could ace [NOTE: Ace meaning I passed].

English bored me. I never cared much for sentence structure, spelling and all the proper grammar and rules that govern our fine language. I thought that was why God invented secretaries and editors.

I wasn't into literature. This is one guy who did almost all my book reports based on comic books until I got busted for it. I guess that's why I turned out to be a pretty good creative writer. It's not easy to make a simple comic book sound like an impressive novel, you know.

And I don't even want to talk about math. When God created Eve, He said, "This is good". When God created Andy Smith, He said, "I need to invent the calculator".

I'm a simple-minded guy. I like things in threes. Father, Son and Holy Ghost, three daughters, three up, three down... those are the kind of numbers I like to work with. I love baseball. If you get around the bases, you get one point. It's simple math. I hate bowling. By the fifth frame, I have no idea what my score is. Bowling was invented for accountants to have something to do in their spare – haha – time.

But history? Now that was one subject I could get into. I loved reading the stories about those who traveled before me.

I enjoyed every era, but especially the stories about the roots of this great country… the good old U.S.A.

How inspired was I reading about those early settlers and how they would start each day before the break of dawn and work so hard through the day performing the chores that developed the character and backbone that would become the very fiber of this great country. The blood, sweat and tears that would turn this virgin wilderness into a prosperous homeland.

When the sun went down, their work still wasn't done. Our forefathers would burn the late-night oil putting their handyman skills to the test in their humble homes. Bedtime would come in the quiet hush of the late evenings, only to rise again before the sun and do the whole thing over again- every day – seven days a week!

You never saw a perky frontier man running around saying 'TGIF!'

And though this all sounds very inspiring to me, there is one question that constantly hounds me as I read this stuff.

How did these people get up in the morning?

They had no alarm clocks in those days, so how did these people get up before anyone has a right to?

Think about it.

These people did more work in one day than I do in a month… and I'm giving myself a lot more credit than I deserve. An 18-hour workday was a short day for these guys. And this was not sitting in some cubicle in corporate America, folks. This was before John Deer was around, ya know. They worked their fannies off. Hard, physical labor that would have me in a coma for months. And they did this EVERY day. No days off. 5-6 hours of sleep then they got up before the sun and did the whole thing over again?!?!

I've asked some history buffs how they did this without alarm clocks and all I get is some silly notion that they had internal clocks or something. Like some crazy desire to get up and get to work again.

So I'm suppose to believe that these people went to bed in the wee hours of the night actually excited about getting up in a couple of hours and start the whole thing over again?

Give me a break!

Most people I know become violent when their alarm clocks go off after eight hours of restful slumber. And they work in a world of air conditioning with laws and rules that actually limit their work each day.

I know it's a small thing to get worked up about, but it's something that has bothered me for a long time. It's hard enough for me to imagine how these people got through the day without TVs, VCRs, Telephones and Microwaves. But they simply could not have survived in those conditions without alarm clocks.

I mean internal clocks and desire?
Get outta here!

Just A Thought

Tragedies Open Heart

Often the question is asked.

How could God let something like this happen?

The answer of course, is another question.

How could WE let something like this happen?

God weeps with us, make no mistake about that. But as we so often do in times like this, we have to point the finger of blame at someone... some country ... some ideology ... some God.

I guess we take comfort in being able to say that others who are 'different' from us were responsible for such a horrendous act of hatred.

We will forever more remember what we were doing on that awful Tuesday morning, September 11, 2001.

We will all have stories, some sad, yet some uplifting. We will all embrace this time as one because we have all shared and been touched by this event.

I have three daughters who are young adults. When I talked to them on Tuesday night, they shared with me a deep fear and sense of insecurity that I had never heard in their voices before.

I told them that now they could appreciate what I felt on the week when my President was shot back in 1963.

Of course an hour later, my mother said the same thing to me about Pearl Harbor.

Sometimes the world puts on its' ugliest face.

Those of us who are decent, compassionate people are overwhelmed with fear and insecurity in not knowing how these moments of grisly behavior will change our lives. And these moments will change our lives.

I spent many years as a counselor working with people who suffered from depression. One of the common mistakes people with depression make is to close down their hearts. I refuse to feel pain. I refuse to feel any guilt. I refuse to feel any more fear.

Though their history might justify this approach, the reality is that the human spirit will never heal with a closed heart.

Our emotions are not like a Sunday brunch buffet. You cannot pick and choose what emotions you want to indulge in. If you refuse to feel pain, fear and guilt, then you must understand that you are also refusing to feel love, peace and happiness.

You can't have it both ways.

During this time of tragedy in America, the answer for us is not to close down our hearts but to open our hearts even more. Now is the time for all of us to open our hearts and feel the pain, the anguish and despair. Yes, we should feel the anger, revenge and contempt for those responsible.

But let us also trust our hearts.

Let us trust the human spirit and understand that we are created in Gods image and in so being are created in- and for- love.

We are good people and as we open our hearts, we will get through the murky waters of despair and find our way back to a stronger and more fervent passion for the life that we have been given.

I have been through many valleys before – both personally and as a member of this great family of life. I have learned that as I open my heart to the moment and feel the emotions in their purest, most honest form – no matter how horrific it may be – I will also open my heart to become more sensitive to all the positive energy that rises from the ashes of pain.

I have cried a lot of tears this week.

I have felt a lot of pain for my family America.

But through the pain and falling tears, I have resolved in my heart to become more steadfast in my pursuit of love and kindness towards all my fellow citizens.

We can blame whomever we want. We can bring them to justice, certainly.

But to me, the answer has always been to embrace and understand the benefits of diversity. I thank God for the diverse world He gave us full of so many diverse people. It makes this wonderful adventure we call life such a

worthwhile undertaking – even when it does show us its'
ugly face.

Love does conquer all!

But only with open hearts.

Just A Thought

Spontaneously Delighted

Routines. This is the mantra for the beloved aging of our world. Everything becomes so routine that it becomes impossible to decipher between what is daily routines and what is sleepwalking (you seldom hear doctors talking about old people and sleepwalking. It's always younger people. Curious?).

If I drop something on my carpet on Thursday morning, I immediately plunge into panic mode – Oh my God, I have two days until I vacuum the floors and it's going to be a lot of pressure to remember to walk around this until then… God I hope I don't have any guests on Friday… Boy, if I keep walking over that it's going to get ground into the carpet and be impossible to get up.

As you age, your brain just works that way. Younger people would respond: Gee, I spilled something. The vacuum is less than ten feet away in the closet and it will take me less than five minutes to pull it out, suck this mess up and throw it back into the closet – no harm done.

Of course, the aging would respond: Yeah, but then what

do you do on Saturday? Do you vacuum the whole house as normal? Do you skip this room because you already vacuumed it on Thursday? If so, do you now need to vacuum this room next Thursday as well, which would be unfair, because now you're vacuuming two days a week and I'm too old for such things!

Young people are laughing at that comment, while old people are saying, "Good point"

Our routines become so engraved in our lives as we get older that any disruption in the slightest – be it a good thing or not – will throw us into panic mode for many sleepless nights trying to recover.

Case in point.

As you know, I am a baseball fan. There is nothing better than to sit at a ball park with friends and watch a ball game. My son-in-law, Jesse, is a great baseball fan as well. He also is a bartender which means that he has more connections than one of my Dad's plumbing projects (trust me, that's funny).

So Jesse calls me on Saturday and drops the bombshell on me:

Hey Andy, I got four tickets to the playoffs tomorrow in St. Louis – wanna go?

I fell into panic mode. 100 reasons that I should say no flashed before my very eyes.

I can't afford a trip to St Louis.

I finish my laundry on Sunday .

I have to get up and go to work on Monday.

I can't miss that show I watch every Sunday.

I should be home in case Rosemary calls me to say hi, after all – what kind of parent am I anyway?

After about two seconds of this practical posturing, the following words fell out of my mouth:

'Damn Straight, I Do!'

So in the bat of an eye, I turned a perfectly normal routine Sunday into a four hour road trip with Jesse and a buddy of his up to St Louis, to their new ball park to watch the Cards and Mets play a slugfest game in which seven home runs flew out into the stands, and another four hour trip back to Nashville where I finally crawled into bed at 4:30 on Monday morning.

Truly a wonderfully spontaneous experience I will talk about for a long time.

And the crazy thing about all this is that my normally scheduled Sunday routines actually worked out fine. I selfishly broke my normal routines and lived to talk about it! Of course, I'm talking a lot more about my exciting adventure to St Louis with my son-in-law than I am about broken routines, that's for sure.

So much more than going to a ball game with Jesse, this moment in time clearly reinforced the reality that I'm only as old as I let myself be.

Yes I am getting older.

Yes my life is becoming more and more a predictive series of set routines.

Yes I did have a hundred reasons why I should have said no to Jesse.

But I said yes to Jesse and hell no to getting old.

And in doing so, I have rejuvenated my youthful spirit that once again reminds me that routines are fine but having a life means being willing to break those routines and enjoy a little spontaneous adventure.

Gotta go ... it's time to vacuum and I simply can't let that go ....

Just A Thought

Conversations for the Heart

I drove home last night laughing at myself while my conscience was mocking me, calling me an idiot among many other things I choose not to share with you. By the time I rolled into bed, I was smiling and instead of reading my book to sleep, I laid there staring at the ceiling thinking about the past couple of hours.

Truth is, I'm really not an idiot. I'm a Dad.

When you are a parent, you live life at the intersection of Worry and Stress. No matter what age they are or what stage they seem to be going through, you spend most of your waking hours worrying and stressing about your kids.

You think that once they leave the nest, you'll stop worrying about them?

Think again.

Certainly when they get married, you no longer have to stress about them as you pass that duty on to the young, healthy man standing there saying 'I Do', right?

Wrong!

I'm certain that as I lay on my death bed, my very last

thoughts will be something in the area of worrying about my girls.

I have no doubt that God has a special place for parents far removed from him in Heaven where they have no access to him because God is no dummy and knows that all parents in Heaven are seeking him with a laundry list of miracle moments that will insure their children's safety back on Earth – and remove this worrying and stressing that really has no place in a place like Heaven after all.

That's why parents always reflect on the 'good old days'.

I think about sitting on my surfboard at the beautiful beaches of San Diego now more than I did as a sophomore at Hoover High daydreaming my way through another geometry class. I can actually remember that time and marvel at how I could get through the day without worrying or stressing about anything.

So what has churned up all this emotional laughter and mocking in mind?

I took my daughter home last night and we sat in my car and talked for a good hour or more. Actually, I should say I mostly listened while she talked.

Let me just say that the absolute best band-aid for the fragile, neurotic parents heart is a good conversation with your kids.

The topic of discussion does not matter to this discussion because much of my laughter on the way home is in realizing how this discussion has renewed memories of so many other discussions from the past that came dressed in many topics but always had the same result.

The mocking comes in that you'd think that after all these years – after all these conversations, a parent would understand that at the first sign of worry, you need to simply go sit down with your child and listen to them calmly explain why you're an idiot for even thinking that this particular topic warranted any measure of worry.

I was a teenager of the sixties and I can say with absolute certainty that there is no greater high than driving home after one of these discussions with your kids.

I am thankful that I have learned not to beat myself up over things like this. You have to have a pretty strong sense of humor to be a good parent, that's for sure.

The joy comes after the laughter and self-conscience smacking upside the head, when you reflect on the conversation itself and realize that your daughter truly has become a great woman.

That's the payoff.

You can laugh at yourself for worrying too long about too little, but there comes that point when you take the more serious side in realizing that you have done a great job in raising your children to be the kind of adults you knew they could be.

Tomorrow when I go to church, God and I will have our own conversation. I am certain that there will be a lot of smiles during this conversation as I once again come to terms with the simplicity that the best medicine for worrying is a good conversation.

Just A Thought

Icing the Sports Heart

I am a baseball guy. I have used baseball themes in this column possibly a billion times. I use baseball in Sunday School lessons, political discussions, wedding plans and certainly in the overall discussions of the meaning of life. Anyone who has double-digit IQs knows that on the seventh day, God did not rest, he went to a baseball game, enjoyed some peanuts and yelled at the umps.

But being the equal opportunity writer – which I don't have to be, being that it is MY column and nobody has a gun to your head forcing you to read it – I wanted to spend today's topic talking about a sport I never dreamed I would ever spend time talking about.

Hockey.

I know what you're thinking.

Here's a surfer dude who grew up on the beaches of San Diego – truly a Mecca for hockey enthusiasts – dedicating today's column to the wonderful sport of sliding around on ice trying to get the biscuit in the basket.

Oh, this should be good.

But before you bail, let me say that although I am an old man often accused of being set in my ways, I also must point out that I have always encouraged the notion that life is short and one should always be flexible enough to try new adventures as they present themselves.

Hey, I can change.

When we talk about sports, certainly baseball is my passion. But I do love sports. Even those I don't care for, I have a respect for.

I could care less about basketball, but I do appreciate some of the storylines that come out in March Madness.

I'll never be a NASCAR guy, but I do appreciate the skills of driving two hundred miles an hour in a bumper-to-bumper rush hour.

Winter Olympics, yes!

Summer Olympics, not so much.

Football I'm almost done with. I like football because it comes during a great time of the year. The Fall, the holidays, the gridiron… it all fits nicely. But they only play once a week, then spend the next six days over-analyzing and over-killing stories about whiny spoiled brats who likely would be in jail if they had to play by the rules of life that you and I do.

But then there's hockey.

For the record, I have long argued that the fights on the hockey rink are lame – they're standing on ICE with sharp blades on their shoes, for crying out loud! I tried to watch hockey, but I never got it.

They had a strike recently, which did nothing to affect my

life as I knew it. But when they came back the next year, they changed some of the rules. I was told by my hockey nuts that the game was even more exciting because the new rules cut back on all the sissy fights and that I should give it another try.

Being the flexible minded guy that I am – and of course, being that hockey in no way intrudes with baseball time – I decided to give it a shot.

After a few games of skeptical pessimism I can now say with a clear conscience:

'WHO KNEW?!'

Oh don't worry. This is one old surfer dude who is not going to run out and buy any season tickets any time soon for a hockey team, let me be clear on that. But what I'm starting to realize is that when you understand that you do not need to understand hockey, it can be quite a fun evening of entertainment.

I have no idea what icing is – even though it's been explained to me a thousand times.

I have no idea why they made that guy go sit in the box – though I'm told he sinned and he needs to sit and think about it for a few minutes.

I could no further explain the game of hockey to you than I could the origin of the universe.

But that's the beauty of hockey. I finally get it.

The game moves so fast and has so much action involved that you don't need to know that much except that everyone is trying to get the puck into the other guys net. Sit back and enjoy that and don't worry about the rules ... just enjoy the game.

I'm not saying I've found a new passion.

Baseball will always be America's favorite pass time – and I'm a true American!

But hockey is certainly a great way to kill time during the off season.

After all, if it wasn't for this new found enjoyment in hockey, five weeks until pitchers and catchers report would seem like such a long time!

No icing now.

Just a Thought

A Books Shelf Life

It occurred to me out of the blue.

I was just sitting there in my living room thinking and the thinking turned down a road that I never had my blinker on for.

Being that my mind was already going down this road, I decided to simply go with it. Funny thing was that as I traveled down this road I found myself not only liking the whole thought processing, but at the same time I was getting upset.

After all, I'm the Godfather of common sense.

My recipe for any of life's challenges has always been a good dose of pure common sense. If common sense doesn't resolve a problem, then the problem has no business in my life and I should just put it behind me.

I've dedicated most of my adult life to the promotion and absolute commitment to common sense.

So how did I miss this one?

Like I said, I'm sitting there in my living room looking around and killing time as I wait for some inspiration to get up and do something other than sitting there looking around and waiting to be inspired. I noticed a small gap in my bookshelf and instantly remind myself that I have to check with my son-in-law about a book I loaned him and remember to get it back when he's done.

That's when my mind took a left turn without a blinker on.

So why do you want the book back – you've already read it.

I know, but it's mine and I have a gap there in my bookshelf.

But you're not going to read it again are you?

Well no – I'm surprised I read it once.

So why do you want it back?

Because it's mine and it looks good up there with all the other books.

But what if he loves the book and decides to give it to his Dad to read?

Well hey, the writer doesn't make any money if we all keep passing it around!

Libraries do it.

Besides, you're the only starving writer left in the world.

Ok, I don't like this road any more. I want back to my wandering mind.

Of course it was more than just the insensitive comment about being the only starving writer left in the world that made me want to bail. It was common sense at its purist form and I was upset that I was challenging it. I never challenged common sense before this and it really shook me.

"ANDY SMITH CHALLENGES THE VALIDITY OF COMMON SENSE' Next on Geraldo.

After pouting for a couple of hours with common sense continuing to throw this spat back at me, I realized that – once again – common sense was correct.

So I decided instead of fighting it, I was going to change my ways.

I don't want the book back.

In fact, I've pledged to myself any time my family or friends are over and show an interest in most any of the books in my book shelf, they are welcome to them.

I guess we all feel that if we have a lot of books in book shelves around our home it makes us feel intellectual or something. I enjoy reading but when I'm done with a book, I want to start a new one. I never want to go back and re-read a book.

I'm feeling quite liberated now that I've mastered yet another exercise in common sense.

I truly am happy to share these wonderful stories that have been collecting dust so as to make thee look intelligent without any withdrawals surfacing in doing so.

And just think of what I can do with the added space that is no longer cluttered with books.

I may start building models or get into art again.

It's all good – even though I didn't take kindly to the only starving writer comment… though truthfully, I can't think of anyone else off hand, but that's not the point.

Low blow.

I'm sure there's others SOMEWHERE!

Just A Thought

Where Are They

Those who have read my stories know that there is one topic or theme that I have always been compassionate about.

At the risk of redundancy – and possibly some tar and feathers – let me put this down on paper once more.

And I will start it with this question:

Where are the people who get it?

I have stopped my subscription to the local paper.

I never watch the local news.

I seldom watch the national news.

Some would say I'm misinformed. I would suggest that I am very well informed by observing and listening to all the people that cross my personal path every day.

Where is the voice of compassion?

Where is the voice of decency?

Where is the voice of love?

Why is it that the voice of Muslim terrorists loudly proclaims justification for their acts of hatred in the name of their God, yet we don't hear any voice from the Islamic leaders who know this is such a horrible misrepresentation of their religion?

Where are they?

Why is it that we always hear the voice of the conservative right Evangelical Christians screaming in the name of Jesus for causes and campaigns that reflect very little understanding of what Jesus was teaching us or how He lived?

Where are the voices that truly reflect the heart of compassion that Jesus had?

Where are they?

We live in a country where politically correct sound bites far outweigh sincerity and compassion.

There is not one person on the horizon who carries the voice of compassion and decency for all walks of life.

Where are those who speak for the least amongst us, not in the name of good sound bites on the evening news, but in the name of all that's right about living within a community of diversity?

Where are they?

We work in corporations where decent, hard working, considerate people usually get written up or asked to leave while people of questionable character often go home with bonus checks in the name of bottom lines.

Customer service is not an endangered species; it is dead in spite of what any spin doctor wants to tell us.

Some say that marketing people are the most powerful people because they have the greatest influence in our lives. If this is true, then we are in big trouble because the mantra they live by is, 'We don't care'. They don't care how annoying they are to you or how truthful they are; all they care about is product name recognition every time you pull out your wallet.

They don't care how it's packaged – throw it in their mail box, email, roll it over their computer when they try to read a story, take over the bottom third of their television screen, slap it all over their favorite team.

As long as the sacred bottom line grows, they don't care.

I keep looking for people that are sincere, compassionate, decent and loving.

I'm looking for people who embrace and celebrate the fact that what makes us so incredible is the diversity of our being. We are people of such diversity of skills, colors, sizes, shapes and environments. We should be celebrating this diversity and how great it makes us.

Instead we spend so much time and energy criticizing and building campaigns that suggest that we would rather create a world that puts us more in line with monkeys.

If you don't look, eat, talk or behave the way I do, then you are wrong.

Even though I do not read the paper or watch the evening news much, I can still hear the voices – and I don't like what I hear.

Every day, I look for the voice of kindness.

I look for the voice of compassion and sincerity.

I look for the voice that comes from a heart of love.

I know they are out there.

I know they want to be heard.

So where are the people who get it?

Where are the people with the voice we long to hear?

Just A Thought

The Worst Job, Really

I have figured out the worst job that a person could have.

This is a job with enormous pressures.

You have to be ready to respond at a moments notice to go anywhere in the world at a blink of an eye.

You have to be ready to perform a massive amount of calculations with absolute accuracy and have it to your boss ten minutes ago.

You never see these people.

Before they can catch their breath, they are off to another location to do the same thing.

Their job is not to be seen but to make their boss look really good, really, really smart and keep all of us regular people in a state of marvel.

Of course, I'm talking about these super accountants who are always the first ones on the spot, calculators in hand, whenever a disaster happens to give us an accurate figure of how much money it's going to cost.

You've seen their work on the evening news: A 6.8 earthquake hit California creating 247 million dollars worth of damage…. a hurricane slammed into Florida causing over 136 million dollars worth of damage… Flooding in Missouri causes 83 million dollars worth of damage.

Oddly enough, how many people die from these disasters comes after the dollar mount, but that's because you can't put a dollar figure on a life, they will tell us, and it's really more of a personal issue after all.

Of course being the logical person that I am, I can't help but think there is a way they came to those figures, right? Some poor accountant was the first one on the spot with his calculator flying out figures faster than you and I could comprehend.

Ok- on this block, there are eight palm trees down … you can get those at Joes Wholesale Nursery for about 25 bucks…. God will water them for free and the city will fertilize …. Wait, wait … ok, hold on here … the palm trees are going to be the responsibility of the government, so they are not going to go to Joes, they will get their palm trees from Harrys Government Gouging Nursery at about 250 bucks per …

And that's just one block, people!

They have to cover the entire area damaged and get those figures off to the networks before air time.

On the up side, these accountants are very popular speakers for the Plastic Pocket Protectors Association Conventions every year.

They are like rock stars.

But they often have to get their banquet dinners to go.

We never question these stories brought to us by these super star accountants. Nobody EVER questions an accountant – even a bad accountant has their fingers flying on a calculator at such speed that nobody ever knows for sure if they are even close to hitting the right numbers. We just figure anyone that dedicated to numbers must be right after all.

That's what they teach you in accounting school – just be fast and they won't question the results!

We are a funny group.

It seems we make money so important that it's the very first part of the story of any disaster.

What did it cost?

As if that figure will determine how much emotionally involved we will be.

If we started every story with …. Today a hurricane slammed into Florida causing twelve people to die… most of us would turn the channel saying, "I don't have no relatives in Florida, so it don't matter none to me"

But when they start out with … Today a hurricane slammed into Florida creating 234 million dollars worth of damage, we become glued to our sets and run to every web site possible to see what we can do to help.

Just seems a little odd to me… a priority thing, I guess.

But I don't think I'd like to be that accountant, that's for sure.

Seems like a stressful job to me.

Just A Thought

Touchdow NASCAR

Now that the NFL has become a 10 billion dollar industry, Commissioner Roger Goodell recently stated that his goal was to reach 25 billion dollars by 2027.

Being the astute sports observer that I am, I will go out on a limb here and say that not only will the NFL not reach this lofty goal, but by 2027 they will be looking back at these 10 billion dollar days as the 'good ol' days'.

I will go one step further in my insanity by saying that by 2030 – if trends remain as they are going now – the NHL will replace the NFL as the winter sport people want to go see.

Not only does that sound crazy, but I will also say that I base this belief on observing a sport that I truly could care less about and seldom watch – NASCAR!

WHAT?!?

My daughter has a son who is just under 2 years old. She is a big sports fan, a track star in high school, commissioner of the fantasy football league, an avid hockey fan and has become a great baseball fan as well.

She states without hesitation that her son can play any sport he wants – except football.

I have three daughters who have many girl friends, many who are young mothers, and I can say that my daughter's sentiment is consistently repeated by more and more young mothers.

Make no mistake about it my friends, a wise man never bets against the comments of a mother regarding her son.

You can say what you will about NASCAR – and again, I am not a fan – but they absolutely understand Moms.

People love to go watch race cars speeding around in circles and openly admit that a big part of the thrill is watching the enormous wrecks that send car parts flying in every direction. Going 200mph with mere inches separating you from other cars in every direction certainly satisfies the thrill factor.

But even the most avid NASCAR fan does not want to see their heroes carted off the track only to be pronounced DOA moments later. NASCAR has always had a good safety record, but when they lost Dale Earnhardt, they took it up a notch.

Now not only is the sport safer, but it has become more popular than ever because fans enjoy watching those huge wrecks even more now with the drivers crawling out, running across the track flipping off the driver who bumped them into the wall!

NASCAR gets Moms …. the NFL does not.

The NHL is just behind NASCAR.

They, too have worked hard to increase the safety of their players to a point that even though it is a much more violent game than football, you rarely have games stopped for injuries. Their protection of players has in no way taken away from the excitement of the game for the fans.

The NHL gets Moms …. the NFL does not.

In the NFL, the games are becoming frustratingly slowed down by a constant parade of injury time outs.

You can clearly tell the gender of the player because – unlike NASCAR and the NHL – the protective padding in their uniforms have decreased in the name of getting that slight edge in speed.

And no fan – especially young mothers – want to see the football heroes of yesterday barely able to walk without the aide of canes.

The NFL talks a good game, but fans can clearly see that they do very little to protect the players of today and their track record clearly shows they do very little to help the heroes of yesterday.

The NFL simply doesn't get it.

Enjoy the mountain top while you can, Mr Commissioner.

My advice to the owners would be to sell your teams now while you can get a ridiculous price for them, and buy yourself a hockey team or race car.

Mothers knows better than this commissioner, I assure you!

Just A Thought

The Signs Are Clear Now

It's been a weird summer, that's all I'm saying.

While the middle of the country was drowning in an assault by mother nature, I'm sitting one door over in Tennessee with sagging spirits from more days without rain and temperatures over 100 degrees than at any other time in history.

Every day the news has stories about weather related events that came with phrases of ... the worst ever .... record breaking ... unprecedented ... on and on and on.

Makes you start to think that maybe Al Gore is right? This Vice President with a personality of a scoop of vanilla ice cream who couldn't even beat that goofy guy from Texas in 2000 could actually have been right?

Well there's one sign the Second Coming is drawing near.

All these brainy people who have Mother Nature figured out are really ticked off. I hear class-action suits against Al are just a matter of time.

These are the people who smugly tell us every summer that .. 'You know this heat means we're in for a rough winter' ...

and then they again smugly proclaim in winter that … 'You know this cold weather means we're in for a hot summer'.

And nobody ever challenges them with the logic that if that were true, then our weather patterns could NEVER, EVER change!

After all, these are smart people and who wants to argue with smart people?

Al better have a good lawyer, I'm thinking.

But there are more signs out there.

Be it the weather, the on-going wars, terrorists making our lives miserable, famines and genocides and of course Apple knocking $100.00 bucks off their iPads ….this is one writer who thinks Jesus Christ is right at our front door and we better start packing people!

Being the community service type of writer, I of course think about the bigger picture.

If Jesus does come soon and takes away all the good folks, do we have an exit plan?

Come on people, we learn from history and we can see clearly that President W had a great plan for going into Baghdad and kicking Saddam's butt, but there was no plan for what to do after that!

For years now, we've been running crazy around the desert trying to figure out how to get out of this God-forsaken desert while a bunch of loser terrorists who can't get a date blow themselves up taking with them many innocent people – so they can go to Heaven and get 30 virgin women.

That my friends, is not a very good exit plan.

We are pretty good about making plans.

We have a plan for fires, earthquakes, tornados and snow.

We have drills at work, school, church and home that will cover ourselves under every scenario the world has to offer.

But nobody has a plan for the Second Coming?!

Are you kidding me!?!

What do we do with the property of those whose entire family is taken away?

What about the property of the churches?

How do the insurance companies handle all the claims?

Is there a form for missing persons that include rapture language?

Do we have any plan of containment for those smug right-wingers who assumed they had front row seats on the freight train to Heaven when they realize that the train has already left the station without them?

This could get ugly fast!

The good news is that there should be plenty of Congressmen and Senators around to form an investigation into this whole mess.

It may take some time, but I'm confident that they'll come up with a thirty volume memo detailing every step of the post rapture procedures that nobody will be able to understand but will clearly benefit all the Congressmen and Senators left behind.

For me, I'm not too worried about it.

I don't think Jesus wants to come back.

In fact, I'm thinking since there hasn't been ANYBODY

who has left this planet and come back, there must be enough on the other side to suggest we don't really have it as good as we think.

People leave and stay gone.

It's not rocket science people.

I'm a good Catholic boy you know, and I feel that if Jesus wants to come back and take us all home early, He's more than welcome.

I'll gladly sit in the back of the train with all the homely people who never got a fair shake in life.

No problem.

My concern is that I have had no luck with women on this side and if all these terrorists are snagging up all the virgins on the other side, then I am going to be one whiny writer, that's for sure.

Please God, show some hope for this lonely old Catholic boy.

PLEASE…. come-on … you made Al Gore look like a genius, for crying out loud.

Give me a break!

Just A Thought

The Big 5-Ohhhh

Turning 30 was okay.

You feel like you're in the mainstream of life. An adult with a career well on it's way to disappointing your dreams.

The 40s were pretty cool.

People in their forties don't care anymore what people think of them. They are done brown-nosing and playing the corporate games of scrambling to get ahead of the next guy. People in their forties pretty much take life in stride. They use their experience to make the most of every situation, but don't get too worked up if things don't go exactly as planned.

After all, some of that experience is in learning that life isn't always fair. I think people in their forties are cool.

Now turning 50 is another story.

For the first time in my life, I'm praying that no one remembers my birthday.

I don't want to turn fifty.

I didn't ASK to turn fifty.

There is nothing about turning fifty that I find attractive in the least bit.

People who turn fifty begin to think about things like whether they could make it if they cash in on an early retirement plan.

People in their fifties keep an eye on their 'portfolio' and stocks and talk about their grandchildren.

They actually pay attention to these commercials that talk about supplemental insurance plans, Viagra, and retirement communities nestled in the quiet foothills of nowhereland!

I'm in BIG trouble!

I'm turning fifty this month and I'm still trying to figure out what I want to do when I grow up!

Actually, I never intended on growing up.

I always wanted to just be a writer, and although I've certainly enjoyed everything I've created, I have not had much luck in being able to quit my day job.

So I'm thinking as I turn fifty, that there is a lot of stuff that I've been missing out on that other fifty-year-olds take in stride.

I'll list them in no particular order because that takes too much thinking and I'm too old to be thinking that much.

I've never used a cell phone or a beeper, and don't even know how they work. I have an answering machine at home and am pretty good about returning calls.

When I'm out and about, I give my full attention to whatever I'm out and abouting for.

The last video game I played was Pac Man and Pong.

Computer games begin and end with solitaire.

I don't even own a camera, let alone a video camera.

I've never traveled over seas.

Heck, my list of things to see in America is still very long.

I have not been much of a traveling man.

I've never owned a home.

I have always maintained solid stature in the Starving Writer's Society.

I've never been in the military.

I've never been in jail.

I've never shot a gun or even held one.

I've never been in a fight or hit anyone with my fist.

I've never been fishing, hunting, or on a safari.

The list of animals I've never seen (outside of cable shows) is too long to list.

I've never been on a farm or ranch.

I have no idea how Wall Street works. Never understood stocks.

I've never got a bill and paid it off without a second thought.

I've never counted my calories, have no idea what my cholesterol level is, and I don't even know how much I weigh.

I've never been picked up by a lady with romantic desires.

I guess as I turn fifty, I could go on and on about the things I've never done, the places I've never seen, and the experiences I've never shared.

But as you get older, you learn to appreciate the things you have and not dwell on that which you have not.

I am the father of three of the greatest ladies ever presented to this fine planet.

That in itself makes me the richest, most traveled and most accomplished man ever created.

I'll leave it at that.

I feel a lot of pressure now to try and figure out what I want to do with my life.

My GOD, I'm turning fifty!

Just A Thought

The Least Amongst Us

As we sit and watch the developments of the aftermath of Hurricane Katrina, we all are asking who is to blame? We are the richest, most advanced country in the world and it baffles us that we can't even respond to our own people in a time of crises.

Emotions run high.

Fingers are being pointed in every direction.

All of us have an opinion.

No matter what religion you believe, I can guarantee you that every religion follows one very basic principal: treat others the way you want to be treated.

You will be judged by how you judge others and let there be no mistake about it, the measuring stick is at the bottom of the food chain, not the top.

You may be a fine, generous citizen, but let me hear your thoughts about those who struggle in the world and that will tell me who you really are.

You may have a nice church and fill your Sunday School classrooms every Sunday, but let me see what you do when one of your members falls on to bad times – whether their own doing or not – and that will tell me what kind of church you are.

You may be the most powerful, wealthiest country in the world, but when you pool your resources together in a crisis plan, let me see what that plan holds for the least amongst us and that will tell me if you even have a plan worth acknowledging.

What happened in New Orleans should make all of us in America feel ashamed.

As a country, we made a plan for the haves, yet we failed to have a plan for the have-nots.

Since 9/11, we have planned and re-planned our response to terrorist and natural crisis situations.

Four years later we clearly see that we developed a plan that responded to everyone but those who need it the most.

It truly is a national embarrassment.

It is not a race issue, it is a wallet issue.

There was a plan for those who are living the American dream, be they black, white, old or young.

They will get back to their homes, rebuild and I am certain that Louisiana – as well as Mississippi and Alabama – will come back greater than ever.

But there are so many who are unable to live that American dream.

They barely get by living paycheck to paycheck- if they GET a paycheck.

They live in a world where a simple flat tire can throw

their ability to keep current with their bills right out the window.

For them, there was no plan.

They simply got screwed.

Should we blame the President?

Not necessarily.

But we certainly should be disappointed in his lack of outrage in what has happened.

We certainly should be furious at all those who are in a position to do something who spent most of their time trying to cover the failure with excuses instead and showing anger and contempt at how poorly our plans responded to our own people.

We should all feel a real sense of sadness for anyone who doesn't look at this whole situation without getting upset.

We are the greatest country in the world.

We will do the right thing and get those communities that have fallen back on their feet again.

We will work hard to insure that this failure does not happen again.

We are America and what makes us great is our history of pulling together as a nation during difficult times.

We have done so for over two hundred years.

But let there be no mistake about this. What Katrina showed us is that our President, FEMA and all those who were put in charge of coming up with a plan failed measurably in understanding how to develop a plan successfully.

The foundation for any emergency plan must give top priority to those who do not own cars, live paycheck to paycheck and have little resources or are laid up in a health care facility unable to respond on their own.

Start with them and build your plan from there and you will have a plan to be proud of.

We failed ourselves this time.

Let's stay mad enough to make sure we don't ever let this happen again.

We are better than this.

Just A Thought

The Legend of Halloween

I was looking through some old notes at a candy factory, trying to get some background history for a story I was working on, when I stumbled across these minutes from a board meeting many years ago.

YOUNG EXECUTIVE: Mr. Chairman, I've been working on a new campaign that might take us out of our current slump.

MR. CHAIRMAN: Well let's hope so... what have you got?

YOUNG EXEC: Well sir, after reviewing the calendar very closely, I realized that October doesn't have any holidays to identify with.

CHAIRMAN: What about Columbus Day?

YOUNG EXEC: Yes sir, well the people down in marketing find that a tough holiday to generate excitement over, since most everyone knows Chris wasn't the first guy here.

CHAIRMAN: I see...go on.

YOUNG EXEC: Well I came up with this idea, see, that

maybe we could start a holiday on October 31st to celebrate witches, goblins and ghosts.

CHAIRMAN: Witches, goblins and ghosts?...a celebration?...and this will help us?

YOUNG EXEC: Yes sir.. .please.. .stay with me here...you see, we have all the kids dress up in costumes.. .you know, ghosts and goblins.. .heck, they can be whatever they want to be...well then they go around to all their neighbors, knocking on their doors...when the people answer the door, they say, "Trick or treat!" and the people give the kids some candy.

CHAIRMAN: I'm missing something, here...On October 31st, we tell the kids to dress up like monsters, go around scaring the hell out of their neighbors and they'll get a bunch of candy?

YOUNG EXEC: Well it's all done in innocent fun... they're not really supposed to scare the people.

CHAIRMAN: I see... I guess...But why a holiday on October 31st?

YOUNG EXEC: Well sir, you see, the next day is All Saints Day.

CHAIRMAN: All Saints Day?...Now you've really lost me.

YOUNG EXEC: Well our research shows that holidays do much better when they are connected to religion.

CHAIRMAN: Of course...Monsters, ghosts and goblins...followed by All Saints Day... and where might the connection be?

YOUNG EXEC: Doesn't matter.

CHAIRMAN: Doesn't matter?

YOUNG EXEC: No sir... Heck, we developed the Easter Bunny to promote candy sales at Easter and it has nothing to do with the resurrection... we developed the jolly old fat man with flying reindeer, and that had nothing to do with the baby in Bethlehem.. .Yet through the years, people have been coming up with all kinds of legends to connect these promotions with the religion. We're confident that the people will also build a connection between Halloween and All Saints Day.

CHAIRMAN: I see...and you're certain that this will boost our sales?

YOUNG EXEC: You bet!...We've got Christmas, Valentines, Easter... then we slip a little during the summer 'cause too much of the stuff melts and gets all messy... this would be a great way to pick up our sales again after the summer. I'm very confident that this holiday will really take off for us.

CHAIRMAN: I don't know...ghosts, goblins and All Saints Day... It doesn't make much since to me.

YOUNG EXEC: And that is why it will work, sir. None of the holiday promotions make any since, and they last forever because year after year, people will come up with new stories and legends of where these promotions came from. As long as we keep quiet and sell the candy, there's no reason why Halloween can't become one of our biggest promotions.

CHAIRMAN: Hmmmm.. Almost sounds crazy enough to

work...Halloween... give candy away to kids dressed like monsters...All Saints Day...Why Not!

And all the time I thought that these holidays were built on legends and religious significance...Ho, Ho, Oh.

Just A Thought

A Costly Education

Boy am I mad!

This is supposed to be the most exciting time of the year for me.

Not because football season is starting and my favorite team is poised for another futile run at the Super Bowl.

Not because baseball is winding down and the ever exciting playoffs are just around the corner.

And not because those dreaded dog days of summer are showing a hint of Mother Nature's own Fall Classic.

Simply put, the kids are back in school.

Yes, getting the kids back on the bus after a muggy summer of "Daddy I'm bored" has always been the big event of the year for a parent.

At least, it used to be.

Parents today are getting ripped off, and somebody needs to stand up and say something about it!

When I was a snotty-nosed kid, my parents would buy me a new pair of jeans, maybe a T-shirt or two and that was that. Once the old yellow bus dragged us off to our wacky world of lower education, my parents were free and clear. For the next nine months, the only obligation for them was to make sure that I at least made a humble attempt at doing my homework before I headed out to play a game of baseball with my buddies.

Today's parents are not so lucky.

Oh sure, it's great to get a break from those "Daddy I'm-bored" routines, but as soon as the children start back to school, we parents are faced with one of the most horrifying assaults of modern time.

Every day our children bring home memos with that most dreaded of opening sentences... "DO TO THE CURRENT BUDGET RESTRICTIONS...."

Five dollars for a workbook.

Two dollars to help pay for gas during an up coming field trip.

Three dollars to help pay for holiday parties during the first semester.

A buck and a half for supplies for a class project.

After a few weeks of this nickel and dime beating, they drag you into a PTA meeting where they announce this year's blockbuster fund raising campaign.

Let me tell you something about this school fund raising campaign stuff.

I get just a little bit nervous when our schools put more emphasis on door-to-door salesmanship than they do exposing the children to the creative arts. When these kids are adults we'll have more Fuller Brush and Encyclopedia salespeople than we'll know what to do with, while our concert halls lie silent!

There are wonderful prizes for the classrooms and the individuals to motivate these youngsters to learn the fine art of being closers.

And of course, we all know who does most of the selling.

Parents!

By Thanksgiving, my co-workers avoid me like a baseball team does a pitcher who is taking a no hitter into the eighth inning.

By the time Christmas roles around, we parents have exhausted our educational financial obligations to such a degree that playing Santa Clause becomes an exSCROOGE-iatingly painful experience.

And as if this is not enough, there is always those people who think that we parents should have to pay for all this stuff.

Why should taxpayers without children have to support these schools?

Fine -Then why not carry that idea into the military? Let the taxpayers pay for all the planes, tanks and ships, and let the families of the soldiers pay for the uniforms, bullets and gasoline.

Or how about the prisons? Taxpayers pay for the cells, family members of inmates have to pay for clothing, food and all entertainment.

Well this is one parent that is sure grateful the World Series and Football games are on TV.

I sure can't afford to go anywhere.

Just A Thought

Out of Respect

As most of you know, I am not a military guy.

As I look at history, I find it utterly ironic how many wars we have created in the name of God, whom I have always been lead to believe is the Author of Love.

I don't pretend to understand the military way of thinking.

I have not had one moment of desire to be a part of the military life.

268 is my favorite number because that was my draft lottery number that basically told me that even if the war came to the beaches of San Diego, Uncle Sam still didn't want me and I may want to take my surfboard somewhere else for a while.

I was totally grateful for that, and have always appreciated that after 50+ years of hanging on this planet, I still have never held a gun in my hands.

So you would think on a beautiful Memorial Day, you'd find a guy like me playing at a beach, cooking some burgers on a grill or simply having fun with my family and friends, celebrating three glorious days of not having to go to work.

"You never win a war with a guy like Andy Smith on your side."

I say that a lot when the conversation moves towards war stories. It takes me out of that conversation with a chuckle and without engaging in any political debate.

Truth is we have won many wars with people like Andy Smith on our side. We've lost some wars, too.

I imagine – and hope – there are many people who never wanted to point a gun at someone else and end their life simply because they were wearing the wrong uniform.

Duty called ... they answered.

They wanted to be teachers and lawyers, firemen, baseball players, nurses and doctors.

They never dreamed of being a hero, they dreamed of being a Mom or a Dad.

Their hope was to live long enough to be a grandma or a grandpa.

None of them started the war.

Many of them probably didn't know who did or even why this war was necessary.

None of them ended the war – the war ended them along with their dreams.

Duty called and they answered.

Some came home in a metal box. Some are buried beneath a white cross in a foreign land. And some simply never came back.

In many ways, these are the lucky ones.

Some came home to wars of their own, having to learn

how to get through life with the broken limitations that only being in harms way can bring you. The physical scars with pain that will challenge them every day.

The emotional scars of watching so many die in such violent circumstances.

Their wars may never end.

I am not unique in my desire to stay out of wars.

God did not favor me by keeping me out of harms way.

I'm just lucky.

I will never understand war.

I will always believe that there is a better answer than conflict.

I will always believe that God is the author of Love and has never made war a part of His will.

I will never apologize for my passive attitude or my heart that faithfully clings to the mantra, all you need is Love!

I'm not going to the beach today.

I'm not cooking out or visiting my family and friends.

Instead of my daily walk around downtown, I'm going to get in my car and drive to the other side of downtown to where they have the plaques and memorials dedicated to the many that have died in the many conflicts of war.

Not because I understand.

Not because I agree.

Simply out of respect.

They wanted to be teachers and lawyers, firemen, baseball players, nurses and doctors.

They did not give their lives for freedom – their lives were taken away by war.

You never win a war with a guy like Andy Smith on your side?

Sure you do….. You also lose them.

I don't agree with the life of the military.

But I do respect those who served.

Just A Thought

It's All About the Game

It's that time of year again folks.

Down the road a piece, baseball players are busy dusting off their gloves and getting ready for another summer of America's favorite pastime.

Another baseball season is upon us and I thought it would be nice if I took this opportunity to explain to you just why baseball is America's favorite pastime.

Now I'm sure all sports fans can make a good case on behalf of their favorite sport. I think there is a lot to be said for all sports. Any fan loves a good, well fought competition, be it on a football field, arena or baseball diamond.

What makes baseball number one in the eyes of the sports fan is really quite simple.

It's in the coaches.

Not the people who coach, but the coaches and how they look.

Nothing is more irritating to a sports fan than to be watching a competition between two rough, sweaty, gritty teams when the cameras keep zooming in on the coach who looks more tailored for Wall Street than a sports arena. A sports fan simply can't relate to the starchy, highbrow fashion statements of today's coaches.

Basketball and hockey are the worst.

These coaches look as if they put more time looking into their mirrors than they do their game plans. And after watching some of their games, they could stand to spend a little more time away from their mirrors working on those game plans.

Football coaches are a bit better, but they still put too much focus on the coach and his image than they need to.

I think they should have dress codes for coaches.

They just don't fit in.

In most sports, the coaches become as much- if not more- of the show than the game itself.

But in baseball, everyone wears the same uniform. The only way you can tell the difference between the coaches and the players is with a bit of gray under the cap and usually a major spare tire around the belt.

In baseball the manager goes out to the mound to talk strategy to his players. He goes out to home plate to argue with the ump and kick dirt on his shoes.

In other sports, the players have to leave the field to go talk with their coach. I guess they don't want to mess up their Italian shoes.

Baseball is a sports fan's sport because it keeps the focus on the game, with no side shows. There are no Wall Street coaches on the sidelines, no cheerleaders, no halftime entertainment, and no clocks to waste time over.

When you are a sports fan, it's really only the game that you're interested in.

That's why baseball is the greatest game of all.

I just thought you needed to know that.

Just A Thought

Jimi Hendrix Made Me a Good Dad

Taking my girls to the Pediatrician reminds of the time I went to see Jimi Hendrix.

I know you think I'm crazy, but stay with me here and I'll explain myself.

It was the sixties. A great time to be a teenager and a horrible time to be a teenager's parent.

We were slamming the door on the Leave-It-To-Beaver mind set of the fifties.

And nobody did the sixties like Andy Smith.

I had my brown hippie hat with beads and feathers, paisley shirts with the sleeves that puffed out, bell-bottom jeans with the peace symbol on the thigh, leather vest and my trendsetting black and white saddle oxford shoes. I was a flower child, possibly the coolest dude ever.

My buddies and I would spend many a Saturday night going to concerts.

We saw all the big ones of that era. Joplin, Donovan, The Chamber Brothers, Fish, Cream, and of course my heroes, The Beach Boys.

But the greatest concert of them all was the night we went to see Jimi Hendrix.

It was also the worst.

We got there early so we could take in all the excitement. The stadium was packed with psychedelic people who were almost as cool looking as me.

Actually, I never could make up my mind if I wanted to be a surfer beach bum or psychedelic hippie during that time in my life, but that's another story I hopefully will never pursue.

Tickets were hard to come by, so we felt lucky to have this opportunity to see the greatest guitar player in rock 'n roll history.

The first band was okay, but everyone was there to see Hendrix.

It seemed like an eternity of some guy coming out every few minutes to tell us that Hendrix was a bit delayed, but would be here soon. The papers the next day said he was two hours late. As a teenager in the crowded stands, I'd say it was at least a month.

We are talking about thirty thousand plus teenagers who had no concept of patience who by now were so wasted on pot, booze and God knows what else that we were well entertained by the pockets of fights and riots going on here and there.

Then the moment we had been literally fighting for occurred.

I'm not sure if I was excited more to see Hendrix as I was that I wasn't killed in the process of waiting.

But this was Hendrix after all.

As we stumbled to our seats, or some proximity to that, Hendrix pulled into the stadium in his Limousine and made his way to the stage.

The first song was great.

What this guy could do with a guitar was well worth waiting to see.

Then he played Purple Haze. Simply put, watching Jimi Hendrix play Purple Haze live is one of the greatest experiences you will ever have in rock 'n roll history. It's one of those classic moments that I still brag about today.

After Purple Haze, Hendrix thanked everybody and stumbled off the stage and into his Limousine.

He was off into the sunset before any of us had a chance to come down from our buzz long enough to realize he had just played two songs and left.

My friends and I got out of there quick, as near riot conditions began to emerge from the crowd that had felt they had been short-changed.

I had mix emotions.

On the one hand, I felt cheated as I spent a lot of money only to hear this guy play two songs.

On the other hand, it was money well spent to have the opportunity to hear Jimi Hendrix play Purple Haze live – and it was the 30 + minute version, to be fair.

And that's exactly how I feel every time I take one of my daughters to the Pediatrician.

No matter how early you might get there, you will always end up waiting well beyond your appointed time.

I'm ready to explode every time they call someone else's name. It's bad enough to wait, but when you're sitting there with your child who is feeling miserable, the time comes to a painful crawl.

When they finally do call you in, you find that the actual time the doctor spends with your daughter is about ten minutes, tops.

I always leave the place with those mixed emotions.

On the one hand, I am frustrated at having to take a day off from work to sit there waiting for a doctor who will only spend a few minutes with my sick daughter.

On the other hand, I am grateful that the doctor knew what was wrong with my girl and we can now get her back on the road towards being that bundle of chaotic energy we've come to love.

For some parents, the adventures of taking their children to the Pediatrician is an episode of anxious homicidal contemplation.

But I don't let it get under my skin too much. I had excellent training for fatherhood when I was a surfer dude, flower-powered hippie in the sixties.

I can handle this.

After all, I saw Jimi Hendrix live, baby.

Just A Thought

My Resume of Peace

So today is the last day.

After today, there will be no more dreary faces on Monday mornings.

No more perky 'It's Friday' every time you say 'how ya doin'?' on Friday mornings.

No more living anxiously as your worth is measured by activities completed, phone calls made, money brought in.

No more frustration in having a compassionate heart competing with a corporate business mentality.

When I wake up tomorrow, I will simply be a retired Andy Smith.

The good news about retirement is that you've had so many experiences in life and understand how this all works.

Life is not a time line of on-going experiences. Life has many chapters that have a beginning and an end. You understand that you need to close one chapter before you can fully embrace the next.

To me preparing for retirement is being able to close that chapter of life labeled adult with a good measure of peace.

That's not hard for me, because I'm a guy who never wanted to be an adult in the first place.

I likely became a great Dad because I never had a desire to be the stern, responsible fatherly figure type. If I had a choice on any given day, I probably would have chosen to spend the day at the beach hanging out, surfing and living a life without responsibilities.

I just never understood the attraction to becoming a responsible adult.

So closing the book on this chapter called 'Adult Andy Smith' is not hard for me.

I'm happy to do so, frankly.

But it's not that easy.

The most important ingredient needed to close this chapter of my life and move forward is inner peace.

It's not important what my successes and failures were; it's important that I have an inner peace about my successes and failures.

It would be fair to say that I have had many more failures than successes.

I've been divorced twice.

I've been evicted and homeless.

I have never been an employee of the month or received a promotion.

I tried to make it as a writer and honestly didn't really come close.

If I was keeping score, I probably had more days of frustration and heartache than peace and joy.

I'm guessing I have had more phone calls from bill collectors than from friendly voices calling to say hi.

That's not a very impressive resume of adulthood.

In fact, the word pathetic comes to mind as I laughingly read this resume before realizing 'oh, that's me' ... YIKES!

But I have learned as an adult to appreciate what Jesus said when he told us that God judges us by our hearts. If it's good enough for God, then it's good enough for me.

I can close this chapter of my adult life because I have complete peace in my heart about my life.

I know on paper it looks pretty pathetic, but I was as good a husband as I was a Dad.

I was as good a co-worker as I was a Dad.

I was as good a writer as I was a Dad.

And I was a GREAT Dad!

As I move forward into retirement, I understand that my world will become much more quiet and self-centered. There will not be a lot of interactions with co-workers and customers.

There will be much more 'me' time.

That's only exciting if you truly have peace with who 'Me' is.

I have complete peace with being Andy Smith.

I go into retirement in peace not because I have built a resume full of successes, but because I have built a heart full of love and self respect, knowing that I have always given my best.

Win or lose, I have always stayed true to who I am and

have enjoyed and appreciated how I approached whatever life threw my way.

Truth is that I'm only retiring from job.

My passion has always been Tracy, Kelly and Rosemary and I will never retire from being their Dad.

If my resume of life only states that I was the Dad of Tracy, Kelly and Rosemary then I have total peace about my life, what I contributed to the world and how the world perceives me.

I'll be good at retirement … I have a good heart.

A heart with a lot of peace.

Peace to you as well!

Just A Thought

Grazzing the Salad Bars

One of the more interesting developments in recent years has occurred at your local eatery.

It used to be that when you went out for breakfast, lunch or dinner, you were treated as a special individual with someone there to wait on your every need.

Your wish was their command.

You told them what you wanted to eat, and they prepared it exactly the way you liked it.

It made you feel like an important person every time you went out to grab a bite to eat.

It made going out to eat special.

Then came the Salad Bar.

I think it started sometime in the 70s.

It was originally designed for those people who still liked to see their toes when they stood up straight. You know, around that time when it was posh to be counting your calories. You could go out to lunch with your co-workers and as they stuffed their faces with greasy burgers and fries, you could fill your plate with a head of lettuce with all the trimmings.

A nice idea.

A good way to keep all those people coming through the doors even when they are counting those dreaded calories.

However, as the years went by, these food peddlers got into a one-up-man ship that has really gotten out of hand.

One guy decided to put out some soup with his salad bar.

Not to be out-done, the next guy put out soup, salad and fruit.

Then came the cheese and chips, desserts and machines to refill your drinks.

Well you know where I'm going with this, don't you?

Today you can go into these eateries, pay four and a half bucks and eat all that you want from a long counter bursting with tasty delights.

We're talking about filling your plate with tacos, spaghetti, meat loaf, chicken, pizza, casseroles, you name it.

And now they have these things in the morning for your breakfast needs.

You can stop by your favorite watering hole after work and find a happy hour with tables full of chips, veggies, buffalo wings, and what have you to go with your beer.

I've even seen these salad bar things in Chinese restaurants and they don't even have any salad.

The problem with these all-you-can-eat ideas is that you always feel rushed. You pile your plate until it won' t hold any more, then you frantically cram yourself so you can get back up to the salad bar to get those few items that you were not able to get on the first run.

By the time you leave, you not only are miserable from eating far more than you required, but you also are all tense and worn from trying to get through the entire salad bar.

It has become another battle in our busy world.

That's too bad.

Our meal breaks are supposed to be a time not only to fill up the fuel tank but a time to relax and take a break from the rat-race we have created for ourselves.

But I guess the good news is that it really works out nicely for all those people who have spouses who constantly worry about their eating habits.

When you go home and your spouse asked you if you watched your diet today, you have a pretty good response.

"Yes dear, I only had a little breakfast bar this morning, then for lunch we all went to that meat 'n potatoes place, but I was really good and only had the salad bar. Then we all stopped off at the watering hole to have a quick beer after work."

The hard part is looking excited when she tells you how she worked hard to reward you with your favorite dinner.

After 20 pounds of scrambled eggs, bacon, grits and potatoes, salad, with all the "trimmings" and a beer with a platter of veggies, shrimp and buffalo wings, it's really hard to get excited about eating a nice pot roast.

Oh well, I think I'll take a break from all of this and go out and get me a good old-fashioned burger n' fries.

Just A Thought

Institution Burnout

Institutions are a good thing.

We need institutions.

We count on our institutions to guide us, protect us and to help us make our lives better.

In many ways, the institutions we belong to reflect the kind of people we are or hope to be.

They give us a sense of security that as long as our institutions are going strong, we feel our lives will somehow always get better.

I'm a big fan of our institutions.

I'm very generous in not asking my institutions to be perfect. I only ask that they keep trying to do the right thing. They don't have to do right by me as long as I can see that they are doing right for the good of the whole.

I'll work within my institutions understanding that I have the ultimate choice for what is best in my life, but respecting the guidelines they give as being a general feel for what is best on whole for a diverse group of broken chromosomes.

Lately, I'm not impressed with the institutions I see. The

people who are involved in the decision making process of these institutions I love are losing control and it's just a matter of time before they either see the light and shape up or they will fall.

Politics: It no longer has anything to do with liberal or conservative, Republican or Democrat, right or left. The people in Washington who have been elected to represent us are nothing more than a complete embarrassment to our country.

The only option I see is if we all refuse to vote at the next election.

I have mentioned before that if they want to reform elections, they ought to put D) None of the above on the ballet so more people will come vote.

I love my country and cherish my right to vote – but I will not vote for someone unless I honestly believe that they are decent people who really do care about what is in the best interest of the citizens as a whole – in other words; I'm guessing I will never vote again.

Washington embarrasses me with their uncivil bickering behavior.

Church: I'm a Catholic. There is nothing I enjoy more than going to Mass every Sunday.

The headlines, however, have been dominated by Priests who have shamefully broken their trust with behavior so despicable I can no longer watch the evening news. The Catholic leadership had better wake up quick or they will be held responsible for the tragic broken lives of so many.

And it's not just the Catholic church – religion as a whole has more leaders speaking words of hate, encouraging behavior so un-Godly or using their position for their own gains and forgetting the people they have been charged to guide.

Again – What an embarrassment our religious institutions have become.

Banks, business, schools, families.

I could go on but the story is the same in all these institutions.

They have become an embarrassment to anyone who has decency in their hearts.

Our institutions that we trust and need have really let us down!

Is there a solution?

God help me, but I never thought I would say this – we need another '60s!

I'm the guy who coined the phrase, 'the '60s is when America threw up!' and I still believe that is a good reflection of what went on in the post Leave-it-to-Beaver world.

But I also think that's exactly what we are headed for today- and I think it's NEEDED.

If you are an honest, decent person you can look around all you want and you will not find any institution that speaks for you.

As individuals, we can no longer depend on any of our institutions to guide us, protect us or stand up for us.

Yes the '60s is when America threw up, but to be fair, they produced a lot of good in doing so.

You can sit in the back of the bus now only if that's where you choose to sit.

If you wear a bra, your paycheck should be equal to a mans if you do the same work.

And though we treated the soldiers terribly, we were absolutely right to scream about the Viet Nam war – and specifically the lying coming out of Washington.

I hope this generation does it better than we did in the '60s however.

We should be angry.

We should scream loud.

But we should be steadfast in bringing changes to the institutions we love and need so desperately with strong hearts for peace, love and a resolve to do right for all people, not just me,me,me.

What we desperately need today is another Martin Luther King jr.

Just don't look for him/ her in any of our institutions, that's for sure.

Just A Thought

When Everybody Wins

Isn't it kinda silly how we've become a society that can't survive without its awards?

You can't go into an office building, business or home without seeing trophies, plaques and certificates collecting dust somewhere.

We've become a pat-on-the-back society, which sounds noble and all, but when you really look at it, there's a lot to be said about the sincerity of all this back-patting.

The entertainment business goes all out with their gala award shows.

You have the Grammy's, Oscars, Emmys, Tonys, CMAs, AMAs, Music Video Awards, Doves, People's Choice, and God only knows what else I've left out here.

They even have a fancy awards banquet for the people who do those commercials that we flip channels to get away from.

Every sport spends its off season handing out trophies and awards to any player who achieved any number of trivial statistics that the computer age sports fan loves to get tangled up in.

And it's not only the high profile tuxedo crowd that gets into this awards stuff.

Go into any work place and you will find plaques proclaiming the employee of the month. Some even hand out a humanitarian award, whatever that might be.

Every day the children come home from school with a fist full of fancy certificates of outstanding achievements for everything from spelling a word right to just showing up to school like you're supposed to.

Now don't get me wrong, here. All these cute little awards and banquets of acclimation are nice.

And yes, they do serve to make us feel good about ourselves and our sense of value in being a part of this crazy thing called life.

But really. All these trophies, plaques and certificates.

All these banquets and celebrated ceremonies of recognition.

There's so much back-patting going on that it's virtually impossible to get through life without attaining some kind of an award along the way – though I honestly admit that I am well on my way to getting through this world with only pictures on my walls.

I'm all for promoting positive feelings and recognition for those who go above and beyond the call of duty, but therein lies the problem.

All these awards mean nothing without merit.

Merit has become one of the most forgotten commodities in our world. It's like baking cookies without using any flour.

Most of us are fully aware that these awards are more the result of popularity than actual merit of achievement. The guy who recently won the Best Actor award for television is certainly a fine actor who has done some wonderful work in the movies, but his TV show is marginal at best and the character that he plays is the same old, same old…week after week…so predictable that you know the whole story within the first five minutes. I love the guy as an actor, but there is no doubt in my mind that he was not the best actor on my TV screen that year.

Unfortunately that story can be ditto'd for all the other award shows.

Year after year.

Even your employee of the month awards are seldom the result of true recognition of an employee who has done something special.

These big-wigs gather around their coffee and doughnuts and carry out the process.

CEO: Fellas, it's time for us to pick next month's employee of the month. any suggestions?

VP: I think we need to choose someone from the second shift. We haven't had one from that shift in a while.

Other VP: How about that secretary who works for Bob?

CEO: Yea, she doesn't seem to bother anyone. Just does her work. Any write-ups on her?

VP: No sir, her file is empty.

CEO: Well, there you go, let's do it. Anyone know her name?

SILENCE

CEO: Someone check it out with Bob and take care of it. Now how about one of those jelly doughnuts?

Awards are nice if they are sincere. If...and only if... they are truly the result of someone achieving something that is special and above the norm. Only if the award recognizes merit more than anything else.

Whether we are movie stars or factory workers, we all generally give our employers an honest day's work for the money.

Certainly an employer should recognize those who are doing all the work. But there are so many trophies, plaques and certificates being tossed about, that they have all but lost their meaning.

They aren't special.

They don't focus on merit.

I always concentrate on producing work that has merit.

The reward is in the finished product...not in some dusty old trophy case.

Just A Thought

Feeling Pete

One of the endearing characteristics of the Gospel story is the people that became the inner circle of Jesus' ministry.

Jesus chose the blue collar people of the day to follow him. These were fishermen for the most part – rough around the edges of life and certainly not your first thought when you think of sending out invitations to drop everything and follow the savior of the world.

But that's why Jesus was the savior of the world and I am not.

He knew the risks involved in choosing these men, but he also knew the benefits.

This is clearly presented in the Easter story.

Throughout the Easter story, it is the women who followed Jesus that remained loyal and steadfast at his side from his arrest to his resurrection.

The twelve men Jesus had chosen to follow him pretty much scattered as soon as they arrested Jesus and were nowhere to be found.

You can't blame them for splitting.

These men were there for all the miracles.

They were witness to the throngs of followers that would come to hear Jesus when he spoke.

They were the ones who were there during all those quiet times and listened to Jesus as he talked about the issues of life.

In what must have seemed like a blink of an eye, this man they had followed was taken away from them by an angry crowd determined to put an end to this radical movement.

I'm thinking I wouldn't stick around either to see how these events would play out.

On the one side, you would have all the followers turning to you asking, "What's next?".

On the other, you would have all the Jewish and Roman leaders turning to you saying, "You're next!"

Clearly, this was not a good time to be Jesus' disciple.

Peter is pure inspiration for a guy like me.

When Jesus was walking on water, it was Pete who enthusiastically wanted to join in and after a few steps started sinking as Jesus had to help him back into the boat.

I like the spirit of Pete.

We don't get a lot, but we get enough to think that Peter must have been a sponge, taking in every word and vision of what Jesus was doing.

I'm guessing he probably would have been the one who drove Jesus nuts with the constant questions during those quiet nights around the campfire.

He was so loyal to Jesus, even to be outraged at the suggestion that he would ever turn his back on Jesus .

I can't imagine the feeling in his heart when he heard the cock crow for the third time.

So when Mary Magdalene came and told Pete that the tomb was empty, it makes sense that he would waste no time in getting out there to check it out.

He had to go see for himself, and when he went into the tomb and saw the linen neatly folded and set aside, Peter merely turns and goes back home, leaving most of us thinking that this is odd behavior for one of Jesus' most loyal followers, isn't it?

Maybe not.

Though it is not clear in any of the gospels, we must assume that what Peter saw was clearly the work of Jesus. Had the burial linens been strewn about in haste, there would always be questions of someone else removing the body. Jesus needed to make clear that this was not the case, and though it is not stated, one needs to believe that Jesus left the tomb in a manner that left no doubt as to what was going on.

If so, it makes sense that Pete would turn right around and head back to his hiding place.

Jesus' followers were looking for him for guidance.

The Jewish and Roman leaders were looking for him in a likely unfriendly manner.

And now the risen savior of the world – whom he denied three times during his most dire hour of need – was out there probably looking for him as well.

I'm thinking Pete was one very uncomfortable person at this juncture.

It all turns out good, however, for Pete and the rest of us.

Thankfully, Jesus is a very loving and understanding savior who knew what he was getting when he told Peter to drop the nets and follow him.

We all take comfort in understanding that the Easter story is not just about a savior conquering death for our sins, but a savior of absolute love who has chosen each one of us – as he did Peter – knowing that we are not perfect.

What a wonderful feeling in Peter's heart later on when Jesus appeared and reassured him that the Easter story would always be a story of love and compassion, not of violence and hatred.

Just A Thought

Bailing Me Out

It's only October and the Christmas spirit is already here!

It has nothing to do with the marketing monsters trying to get a jump on the other guys by jamming Santas down our throats as we shop for Pumpkins to carve.

I'm talking about the real deal here.

There has never been a more generous act of Christmas spirit in my life time.

I mean this act of kindness makes Mother Teresa just look like a nice lady.

Uncle Sam just passed a bill that will have our government buy up 700 billion dollars worth of bad debt. And when you look in the stocking hanging by the fire with care, you will find all kinds of little goodies that we Americans have been nervously holding our breath in the hopes that someone in congress would finally have the balls to help out.

For instance, they had the courage to recognize the struggles of the Rum industry in the Caribbean by giving them a long overdo tax break.

And who wasn't screaming at our leaders to step up and finally give some tax relief to the wooden arrow industry?

This will be the best Christmas ever!

Now you all know I have never been accused of being an economic genius. I never look at statements beyond 'Pay this amount', and I'd rather have constipation for a month than sit down and try to balance my checkbook.

I won't pretend to try and figure out exactly what this whole bail out thing is all about.

I do know that when it comes to government spending, the money is never real. Our politicians just maneuver these dollar figures from issue to issue to give the world the impression that they- the politicians- are doing something, and we are a wealthy country.

All the other countries figure if the United States can give the wooden arrow industry a tax break, well they must be doing pretty good and we should go ahead and keep doing business with them.

In politics, it's all about perception.

I also know that a few years back when everyone was telling me how easy it is to buy a home, I was one of the few who was smart enough to look at the real math of living alone making around 38,000 dollars does not add up to a 150,000 dollar home.

I'll stay in my simple one bedroom apartment, thank you.

So when the government decided to pay off all this bad debt so the banks could give loans out again to people who know not how to live within their means, I was ecstatic. The worse debt is the student loans and credit card that affect my wallet, so I am certain that these are at the top of that 700 billion dollar pay off.

Thanks Uncle Sam!

Now this will free up about 300 dollars a month for me, which may not sound like much to you, but on my salary, this is huge. I'll be able to spend more on some of that Caribbean Rum which makes this all a win-win situation – exactly what the government is hoping for, right?

What a euphoric feeling that will be next month when I get my bill from Salle Mae and CitiBank and can throw those suckers into an envelope addressed to my congressman.

Of course, there will be a nice thank you note with it as I really do appreciate how congress has once again looked out for my best interest (though I'm still a bit shaky on this wooden arrow development).

After all, if I pay my taxes AND pay these bills I'll be paying twice for the same thing, right?

People who foreclosed on their homes didn't pay at all and that's kind of the problem isn't it?

Some think I'm just being silly, but I'm serious here.

I may not be a financial wizard, but I've always lived within my means.

Of course Uncle Sam would want to reward people like me first as an example of how we all should live our financial lives.

I mean if they just bailed out those people who foreclosed

on their homes that they probably shouldn't have bought in the first place, what kind of message is that?

It's a very simple principal of life – you reward the good guys not the bad guys.

Maybe that's what this wooden arrow thing is all about.

Maybe the company is run by a good guy.

Maybe I should use some of that extra 300 bucks and buy a box of wooden arrows to help this guy out, too.

Happy Holidays, everyone!

Just A Thought

Cyber Searching

I got an email this morning that opened my eyes to this wonderful world of computers like nothing ever before has.

Lost in a pile of annoying spam – most of which starts out so politely; 'I'm sending you this crap because I didn't want to bother you with a call…' Thank you, Do Not Call List! – was an email from a man who I played little league baseball with.

Wow – what a shocker that was.

The story is that Sherman Moffitt was featured in one of my columns here on my web site; ' Heroes of my Youth', to be exact.

Well the real Sherman Moffitt decided to put his name in a Google search and he was directed to my web site and the story I wrote about him. He wrote me a very nice email thanking me for the kind words I said about him.

Well you can imagine the possibilities this opened up for this creative writer.

First, I started searching to see if I've said anything stupid or liable about someone in any of my stories that might just come back to haunt me.

But hey, I'm a writer.

I say a lot of stupid things.

I just try to say them in a cleaver way.

I'm not going to get worked up about that.

Then I started thinking that I have to write a story about SALLY JENNINGS. I had a huge crush on Sally. She was a cheerleader at Hoover High and I just thought she had a smile that could melt the North Pole – it certainly melted me.

Maybe if I write more stories about SALLY JENNINGS, she too, would search Google and they would take her right to my site.

Be still my heart!

But I'm thinking inside the box.

I need to use this idea to my advantage (but do expect more references to SALLY JENNINGS in future columns!).

I need to use names that will draw these people using Google search to my web site.

Let's say I use MOHAMMAD ALI in a story?

There has got to be a lot of people who will do a search on Google for MOHAMMAD ALI, right?

Now my friends at Google will send them all to my web site!

How cool is that?

By just writing about MOHAMMAD ALI, my web site goes from 4 hits a year to untold millions of opportunities for people to visit my site!

Now for those of you who are actually here looking for stuff on MOHAMMAD ALI, let me just say that he was a boxer by trade who knew stuff about animals. He talked about Butterflies, Bees that sting and Gorillas. I'm thinking he was quite a nature guy. But hey, while you're here, why not grab a cup of coffee and read some of my stories?

This could be fun!

I just have to work out the right names to use that will draw the right people to my web site.

This could be hard, because dropping names has always been a weak side of my existence. But it certainly warrants my effort if it will get the good people at Google to pitch some people out to my corner of the Cyberworld, that's for sure.

But maybe I'm still thinking too small.

How about this; Yachts AND Foreign Tax Shelter Opportunities.

Wow!

Now the Google people will be sending a bunch of rich people who have money to burn to my very own web site!

This could be the mother load of web site profit potential!

Note to rich people who came here looking for YACHTS and FOREIGN TAX SHELTER OPPORTUNITIES: This is perfect for you – no kidding! Actually, I know nothing about Yachts, but I do have a cork screw for wine bottles and am always up for new adventures should you need a cabin boy of sorts. But if you're looking for a place to hide your wealth, trust me on this. Don't throw your money away on some foreign soil, send it to a real American buddy who will watch over and take care of that money. Starving Writers Named Andy Smith Foundation (SWNASF) is designed with you in mind. The most anonymous writer in the history of mankind, your money will NEVER be found if you just contact me and Ill let you know where to send that check.

My mind is reeling with new ideas for stories now!

Thanks to my old little league buddy, Sherman Moffitt, this is one writer who sees the possibilities.

Oh, and if anyone knows SALLY JENNINGS, please tell her to search Google – I'm waiting for you, Sally!

Just A Thought!

Dream On Joe

I have often wondered how Joseph got through his life without a sleeping disorder.

Every time you read about Joe in the Bible, some Angel is appearing to him in a dream.

Here's a simple guy who only wanted to be a good carpenter, get married to his sweetheart, Mary, have a bunch of kids and take a vacation from time to time to Disneyworld.

Unfortunately, poor Joe kept falling asleep.

First, this Angel comes into his dream and tells Joe that Mary, his innocent bride-to-be, is pregnant, but still a virgin, and that he is to go ahead and marry Mary and get her out of town.

So Joe packs his pregnant, virgin wife off to Bethlehem and helps her give birth to a savior.

Everything seems to be going just fine when one night, another Angel appears to Joe in a dream and tells him that Herod is really ticked off about this savior stuff and he needs get Mary and Jesus the heck out of there!

Sooooooo

Joe packs up the wife and savior and travels hundreds of miles through the boring, hot desert into Egypt where the cranky Herod would not find them.

Well everything seems to be going great for the Carpenter family when, once again, that annoying little Angel crashes Joe's dream to tell him that Herod is dead and won't bother them any more and that they are free to pack up all their cares and woes and head back through the hot, boring desert to a place called Nazareth, Galilee!

Sooooooo

Joe packs up the donkey, who by now is getting really tired of this moving van stuff, and takes the fam back through the boring, hot desert to their new home in downtown Nazareth.

Now maybe I'm a little off base here, but I'm thinking that by the time poor Joe got to Galilee, he must have had a tough time getting to sleep at nights.

I sure would.

His dreaming had certainly turned his simple world upside down.

I would have complained all the way through the desert.

"Hey, God – Don't you have any Angels that work the day shift? I mean, is it asking too much to have your Angels call on me during normal business hours? Enough, already!"

And you know that these dreams took a toll on the marriage.

I can see poor Joe sitting there with his morning cup of coffee trying to explain to Mary how they have to head back through the boring, hot desert again.

I bet those two did some serious entertaining of changing religions.

"Mary, we have got to find a God that will work with us during the days so I can sleep at night."

"Yes, dear, I know. And it would be nice to find a God who will let us stay put for awhile so I can get some good use of my drapes."

Joe's life certainly didn't turn out the way he hoped it would.

But Joe didn't seem like the guy to complain much.

He was given a job and simply went about doing it right.

A good carpenter will do that.

But if there were photographers around during that time, you know that Joe would be the one with the bags under his eyes.

Just A Thought

A Contradicting Word

I have been thinking about the many contradictions that we have in our world.

I think people have turned contradiction into an art form.

People who go to church regularly, suddenly drop out of church when their personal life goes sour, yet people who seldom go to church suddenly head to church when their personal life goes sour.

Go figure.

I know a lot of people who rock 'n roll their fannies off in a thundering 45 minute aerobics class, then go out for pizza and beer to recover.

Football players are the masters of contradiction. Off the field, they are very macho, cool, unemotional hunks with sever personality deficits.

On the field, they jump up and down in excitement, pound their helmets together, hug their teammates, create wild provocative dance routines in the end zone, and make a lot of animalistic howls and calls when their team does something good. Then it's back off the field with their very macho, cool, unemotional sever personality deficits.

Contradictions.

We see them everywhere we go.

You'd be surprised at how much of your day is consumed with contradictions. I can't think of any job that doesn't have a lot of contradiction woven through it.

With all the contradictions we face, I do think that I have figured out what the most contradictive part of our world is.

It's just one word.

Three letters.

And with this one little word, the world becomes a sea of contradiction.

BUT.

Whenever I hear someone using this word, I automatically prepare myself for another contradiction.

"I have nothing against poor people, BUT…." (Don't look for any endearing comments about the poor here).

"I'm not a bigot, BUT…." (Prepare your ears for a loaded bigoted comment)

"I really appreciate you doing the laundry, dear, BUT…." (She thinks I'm a moron because I can never match the white socks right)

"We're really glad to have you working with us, BUT…." (Time to find out how much unemployment you have)

"We checked your car out, Mr. Smith, and everything looks great, BUT…." (Start writing that check…$300 bucks, minimum!)

"I know we told you that it would be ready on Tuesday, BUT...." (Their calendar likely doesn't have any Tuesdays on it)

"As your Congressman, I will never support higher taxes, BUT..." (Somebody has to pay for all my 'fact-finding' vacations, you know)

"We have a lot of good, young talent on this team, BUT...." (Don't save up for postseason tickets this year)

"You certainly are qualified for this position, BUT...." (The supervisor's nephew already got the job)

"I really like your creative ideas, Mr. Smith, BUT...." (A rejection is still a rejection no matter how sweet you try to make it)

"I'm going to do my chores soon, Daddy, BUT...." (Count on the kitchen looking like a war zone by weeks end)

It's just a word.

A pretty small, unexciting word at that.

It certainly doesn't look very threatening on paper.

You wouldn't think of it as having all that much power, yet those three little innocent letters can turn a positive comment into a negative faster than a teenage girl can turn a run in her stockings into an apocalyptic event.

It doesn't seem like much of a word, BUT....

Just A Thought

Animals, Gray Hair and Arthritis

Okay, I admit that some of my favorite shows on TV are those nature shows they show on the cable channels. I really like to watch shows that explain all the wonders of the animal kingdom.

The other night I was watching one of these nature shows when the question hit me;

Why don't any of the animals ever get gray hair, wrinkles and arthritis when they get older?

Think about it.

Most of the time, the only way you know that one animal is older than the other is when the guy with the snobby British accent tells us so.

This really perked my curiosity, so I started going over all the nature tapes that I had to find the answer (yes, I even tape a lot of these shows. Hey, I enjoy watching them when I do the weekly ironing. Wow, I guess that comment really ruins my macho image, but in order to save face, I will say that I also do the ironing during Monday Night Football. I only watch the nature shows during the off season).

Anyhow, after watching a number of tapes of my favorite Lions and Tigers and Bears, I think I finally figured it out.

Animals don't get gray hair, wrinkles or arthritis because they don't have to spend as much time raising their kids as we do.

When an animal has a child, they start right from the beginning to prepare it for a life away from the nest.

In many cases, the child will barely be able to walk, swim or fly when the mother sends them out into a world of independent survival of the fittest.

They don't have to deal with family reunions, birthday get-togethers, Thanksgiving dinners, proms or worrying about Junior keeping up the family name.

Animals for the most part don't have to potty train, keep the China off the shelves, watch electrical outlets, tampered baby food, riding bikes, playground equipment, dating, driving, broken hearts, weddings, or that ever-elusive Jones family that everyone keeps trying to keep up with.

All they have to do is teach them how to eat, and then wish them luck.

Not so, we humans.

No sir, we spend a great deal of our children' s life sticking our nose into most everything they do as if their success in this world will be the only topic of discussion when we turn in our time card to St. Peter on that fateful day of judgment.

Parents are always looking forward to the 'next' stage.

Right from the day a child is born, the parents are always saying the same thing…

"I can't wait 'til Johnny can walk."

'I can't wait 'til Johnny can speak."

"I can't wait 'til Johnny is potty trained."

And it never ends.

Parents will be anxious for the next stage in their child's life until they leave the nest.

The funny thing is that when they do leave the nest, these same parents will sit around and mope.

"They grew up too fast."

"Where did the time go?"

"These kids today mature too fast."

I don't know, somewhere in the Bible it says that we are the greatest of the animal kingdom. I keep hearing that we are so much more superior to the rest of the animal world.

Well far be it for me to drag this into a religious debate.

We are an interesting group of broken chromosomes.

Sure we get too anxious for junior to get to the next stage instead of enjoying the stage he's in.

Sure we probably do make too much over the sillier side of life.

We raise our kids too much out of monetary stature and image within the community instead of from the heart of reaching for that individual star that was created for our child.

I guess the other animals have it a bit easier than we do.

But I'll take the gray hair, wrinkles and arthritis for the opportunity to be there for my children as they grow.

To kiss their owies, lend them my shoulder when their hearts are broken.

To scream at them when they are teenagers and to walk them down the aisle at their weddings.

Heck, if I got rid of my kids as soon as they learned to walk and eat, I'd probably be a better-looking guy today.

But I doubt I'd ever have that twinkle in my eye that I do now whenever I'm with my girls.

I better go get the ironing started.

Just A Thought

Being A Sky Guy

I'm a sky guy.

My girls can tell you how many times I would preach to them about the benefits of looking up.

There's something about looking up to the sky as we hurry off to our cars and busy worlds that really gives our world a proper perspective.

Tonight I took one of my evening walks.

It's the first day of summer, so I know that there will be fewer evening walks in the next few months.

Tonight was just one of those nights.

The clouds have been passing through at a brisk pace today, some dropping off some rain, and others clapping and showing their might as they pass along.

But the sun still prevailed throughout the day.

Muggy, steamy and unpredictable – a typical start for summer.

But as the sun began to fade towards the west, you could feel the refreshing dryness of the front that brought all this activity.

Simply put, it was a beautiful night for a walk.

Comfortable, breezy, and one of the most contradicting skies I have ever seen.

Big powerful clouds. Some dark gray with bright silver lining from the sun. Others just gloomy and threatening with orange around the fringe. All with a rich blue backdrop to provide an even greater sense of contrast.

I could see that my neighbors a few miles to the east of me were not enjoying a nice night for a walk.

As I am walking, a few thoughts cross my mind.

First, I can't help but ask how there could possibly be people in this world that do not believe in God. I've heard all the arguments and frankly, some of them make a pretty good argument for sure. But as often is the case with us, we tend to think too much instead of observe.

As I take my walk, I am absolutely speechless at God's creativeness.

I am amazed at His artistic expression in something so simple as a day's end.

For centuries, our greatest artists have tried to capture this scene on canvas with very limited success.

After all, you can't paint the soft breeze, the birds singing or the subtle thunder of the distant clouds.

But God can.

And He does so nearly every night.

The other thing that I am aware of is how I have made this evening journey and encountered two other people out enjoying God's canvas.

Two people.

I walk for an hour through beautiful neighborhoods with nice houses, big lawns and quiet settings. And on a beautiful night like tonight, I only encounter two other people.

No wonder people don't believe in God.

They're missing Him.

How sad to think that there would be so many people who enjoy the benefits of a comfortable life missing such a golden opportunity that has been afforded them this evening.

I am a baseball fan. Tonight the Red Sox are battling the Yanks on TV. Certainly a game worth settling in to watch.

But as I put away my dinner dishes and peer out my window, I can see that there is much better programming to be embraced out in my neighborhood.

TV will always give us highlights.

God only gives us moment by moment.

It was a great walk.

One that truly made me appreciate the world I live in.

Most of my evening walks do.

It's all about perspective.

As I finish this, I look out my window and see darkness. But I can see the stars sprinkled about the darkness.

Another of God's great masterpieces.

Another example of God giving us the perspective we need in our lives.

People have asked me how I survived the many valleys of my life.

I find all the answers in the sky.

I will always be a sky guy.

One final thought.

Tomorrow when I go to work, I will be able to converse with my fellow baseball nuts about the game on TV last night. Again, they have highlights and I'm well aware that the Yanks beat the Sox in what appeared to be a pretty good game.

However, if I say, "Hey did any of you catch that sunset last night?", I will be surrounded by a bunch of blank looks from people thinking old Andy is losing his marbles.

How sad.

The best shows don't have highlights.

Life is a moment by moment thing.

Just A Thought

The 80 - 20 Factor

One of the worst things that we have created for ourselves is the critic. You know, those people who make a good living telling us what they think about stuff.

We have movie critics, theater critics, art critics, music critics...

The world is full of people who are telling us what we should like and dislike.

I used to think that it would be a great job to have. Just think, I could go to the movies for free and then go on camera and tell everyone what I thought about it.

Pretty nice job, right?

Not only do I get into the movies for free, but I also get paid a generous salary to tell everyone that I thought the movie stunk!

But there is something that really bothers me about these critics.

I learned a long time ago as I started out in the music business that when you work in the creative arts... i.e. – music, movies, TV, radio, art, writing and what have you…you enter into a 80/20 relationship with those who pay the rent.

If I am on stage performing my songs, 80% of the song is what I put into it and the other 20% is what the audience takes from it.

The absolute worse thing I could do as a performer is to stand up there and tell everyone what the song is all about.

It denies my audience the right to their 20% of the song.

By interpreting my songs, I am not letting my audience be a part of my music.

The same holds true in Art, Movies, creative writing and any other form of entertainment.

When I write my columns, I put 80% into formulating an idea and working on a story that I think you would enjoy.

But everybody who reads the column gets their full 20% share by taking my words as they will.

You may think I'm a genius or you may think your paper is wasting a lot of ink on a fool like myself… whatever you think, is fine with me… it's your 20% and I'll respect that.

So I ask myself why then, do we need these critics telling us what we should think about our entertainment?

It's like we are paying these people to take away our 20% of the entertainment market.

Critics are an interesting group.

Theater critics almost never have anything good to say about a show. In fact, in many cases, production crews get nervous and start packing when they get a good review.

Movie critics are a bit too pompous. If they knew half as

much as they think they do, they'd be big time producers in Hollywood instead of small time movie critics on our evening news. Isn't it funny how these critics can destroy a movie, and then a few weeks later, when given the opportunity to interview the star of that same movie, they unload lavish praises for being such a wonderful actor/actress?

Art critics should be politicians. By the time they are done critiquing an art show, you haven't the foggiest idea of whether they liked it or not. You can never interpret their interpretation.

But I guess it's all pretty harmless. I don't think there has ever been a movie, show, record or painting that went under because of these critics.

We pretty much hold on to our 20% of the entertainment business.

Maybe these critics would be better off working in stores. You know, every week they can come on the TV and tell us what they think about the price of corn... or bread, or what's hot and what's not at the local grocery store. I mean we don't have a 20% partnership in the grocery business, so why not let these critics go ahead and do our complaining for us?

I still have to admit that it sure is the best way to get into the movies for free.

Pass the popcorn, please!

Just A Thought

Positively Prioritizing

I like to think of myself as a positive guy.

I approach all my writing with a desire to be uplifting.

If I was a screenwriter, I would have a resume full of sappy, feel-good movies, not horror movies.

If I was a journalist, I would always look for great uplifting stories about the good of people and never consider any investigative reports that bring down people.

I have the most positive keyboard around – no negative letters welcome on this computer, thank you very much.

But today as I look at the world we live in, my story falls under the heading, I hope I'm wrong, but I think I'm right.

I have said many times that when you put money as your top priority, you lose.

Oh you'll get the money, but you'll lose.

Whether you are an individual, a church, business or country, when you make money your top priority, you almost certainly guarantee failure.

Now don't get me wrong – this is the same guy who has said many times that the more money you have, the more fun life can be. I do not believe that the pursuit of money is a bad thing. I'm saying that when it becomes priority number one it is.

It's a mindset.

Generally speaking, wherever your focus and commitment lies, you'll have your greatest successes in life.

Athletes show us this every day.

We see them achieve unbelievable levels and almost always follow it by simply saying that they just stayed focused on doing what they needed to do to win.

Businesses do it all the time.

The themes you hear every day is find more money.

Find more ways to create income.

Meanwhile, they cut back on benefits and perks that mostly affect the front line employees and cover their greed with pointing to the recession as the reason.

Wall Street is not a one way street, it is a global street that reflects the business attitude throughout the world- and it's a pretty greedy, self-serving attitude at that.

It's everywhere.

Government, churches and individual people are all doing the same thing.

It's amazing when a natural disaster hits somewhere how quickly the story becomes how much will it cost and who is going to pay for it.

Now I'm not the sharpest pencil but what concerns me the most is that I don't see a lot of hope.

It's getting worse by the day and I don't see or hear anyone doing anything to stop this madness.

Everywhere I look, the conversation turns to money.

I can't even watch a baseball game without the broadcasters spending at least 2-3 innings talking about players whose contracts end at the end of the year and what teams can afford him and what this team can afford to do if they lose him.

STOP!

What is the answer?

Well the simple solution is to believe that the Mayans are right and on December 20, 2012, God will have had enough and put an end to this little blue ball we've screwed up and let us all go to our eternal rewards as He sees fit.

He does have plenty of other planets to work with after all.

That's the best solution because it means that we only have a short time left of this insanity and it does not require us to do anything – God will stop it for us.

On the other hand, I'm thinking we really do need another '60s.

We need another Martin Luther King to speak up and challenge us all to change the path we are headed.

We need a leader to peacefully fight for the values that we know will provide a better life.

Money is one of the most volatile parts of the life we have.

When you focus on money, it's never enough.

It creates greed, selfishness, chaos and separation.

Relationships are the most stable parts of our life.

When you focus on relationships, you become stronger in character.

It creates community, peace and a more reliable means of surviving adversity.

Seems to me if you are an individual, business, church or government, you'd want to have relationships as your top priority, not money.

With your focus and commitment on relationships, you will always win.

It doesn't seem to be rocket science.

We just need a voice that screams loud enough.

Money is nice for sure.

But hey, if your focus is on relationships and you run out of money, at least you can borrow twenty bucks from one of your pals, right?

Just A Thought

Holiday Fever

Every month it's always something.

One month it's Valentines Day for those who are romantically inclined.

Another month has St Patrick's Day for those who like to drink a lot of green beer for no apparent reason.

It got me thinking about all these holidays.

In most work places, there are about 14 holidays where an employee gets the day off with pay.

That's pretty good.

But if you're anything like me, you can only name a handful of those holidays.

For me it's usually a matter of looking at next week's schedule and seeing that I get next Thursday off with pay. I'm not sure what the occasion is, but if the employer is going to pay me to stay away from work, I certainly am in a celebrating kinda mood.

But as I was thinking about all this, I came up with an idea that would absolutely help the corporate mentality of todays business world, which for me is always a frightening experience.

Why don't we take all these holidays, trash 'em and start all over.

We can keep the main ones, but then let each individual pick the rest for their own personal taste.

If you get a job, the employer gives you 14 paid holidays. Thanksgiving, Christmas, New Years and the 4th of July are automatic.

Everyone gets those.

But the other ten are up to you. Your birthday, wedding anniversary, your first date, the day your divorce became final, the day the bill collectors stopped garnishing your paychecks, whatever.

Everybody has ten days that means a lot to him or her, and little to anyone else.

They should be paid holidays.

Of course, there would have to be some rules.

You couldn't clump more than two of them together. Most of us get at least two weeks vacation on top of our holidays, so anything over two days should be used for that.

You should be able to change most of them from year to year.

My daughter graduates from high school this year. Graduation day would be a good holiday for me.

Next year I wouldn't need it.

Most people get to that age where they would want to

exchange their birthday for something more noteworthy, say, the day the white sale begins at Wall Mart?

And think of how it would benefit the employers.

They would only have to close up shop four times a year.

They wouldn't have so many employees unproductively hung over at any given time.

The mass scramble to finish up work and head for the parties would be limited.

And the financial consequences of paying someone not to show up for work would be more spread out during the course of the year.

You'd think that on an election year, the politicians would forget about balanced budgets, world peace and global warming long enough to deal with important stuff like this, wouldn't you?

But then again, you're talking about a group of people who have twice as many paid holidays as the postal service.

They wouldn't have a clue of what this is all about anyway.

Just A Thought

A Champion At Last

If you are a guy, you have a gene that requires you to spit, scratch and pump out your chest in a show of strength.

I call it the Dork Gene, but I think it's commonly known as the Macho Gene.

Actually I think science has some scientific name for it, but outside of scientists, nobody ever cares what they call stuff, so I'm not even going to try.

The Dork Gene probably came in handy when cavemen had to go get dinner with a stick, but I'm kinda thinking that it's become more of an annoyance over the last two million years than anything beneficial.

Especially in today's world where women carry a much bigger stick and are not afraid to use it, but that's not my story today, so I'm not going to go there.

Most guys are like me.

I love sports but never really excelled playing them.

I know how much hard work and talent it takes to be the last one picked for any game, so obviously I have the utmost respect for any athlete who can go out and play the game with authority and grace.

Guys always fantasize of how they too, could be making seven million a year if they only learned how to hit a curve ball, or fast ball, or learned how to turn a double play, or......
well, it is a fantasy after all.

That's why fantasy football leagues work so well.

In reality, guys like me are looking at best at being a marginal player in a co-ed church softball league.

But in a fantasy football league, you become a general manager of a professional football team, responsible for making all the moves and using your brilliant knowledge of the game to humiliate all your competitors and show the world what a genius you really are .... spit .... scratch.....
pump up your chest.

So the first year I joined a fantasy football league, I did so because my daughter was the commissioner and she needed more teams, so being the good dad that I am, I threw my Dork Gene into the mix with thirteen other teams.

I started the season going 0-7 , which I believe is still the longest losing streak in this league, but hey, it's not MY fault – I didn't go out there and play the game, ya know – stupid spoiled, rich athletes .... spit .... scratch... pump out my chest.

I did rebound nicely ending my first season with a convincing 4-12 record, just missing the playoffs by about eight games.

In the off season, I was sitting there talking to a young lady who was on one of the teams in our fantasy league. She was mentioning how frustrated she was because the guys seldom let her make any moves and next year she wasn't going to be on their team.

I mentioned that she would be welcome on my team since I raised three daughters and have long given up my Dork Gene and… well… given my record I certainly couldn't do much worse.

She accepted and we became Jen & Juiced – her name being Jennifer and my …. well, it is a bar league, after all.

We got together for our draft and I told her the only stipulation I had was that we could not draft any Raiders – being a San Diego Charger boy, I would NEVER lower myself to root for anyone in the silver and black.

She had all her lists and we discussed each choice as a team and before long, she made all the choices that gave us a roster that I thought was pretty decent.

We had no Tomlinsons or Mannings, but we had a good group of players that should keep us in the hunt if they just played to their potential.

Every Saturday morning, I would pull up the league site to see what moves Jen had made for this weeks games.

My first reaction was always, 'What the hell is she doing?', followed by about ten minutes of really looking at her moves and thinking, 'Damn, that's not bad.'

My role became master smack talker, which anyone with a Dork Gene knows is paramount in any sporting event… spit …. scratch …. pump out my chest.

After spending most of the season in the middle of the hunt, Jen & Juiced slowly climbed up the standings, making the playoffs... and last weekend, actually winning the Super Bowl!

Jens moves and my smack talking became the stuff that championships are made of.

I went from pathetic to champion by making the best move of the year – getting Jen- a GIRL without a Dork Gene- on my team.

The guys will always have the need to spit, scratch and pump out their chests as long as they have the dreaded Dork Gene.

But the lesson is that whether it's fantasy or reality, sports are games and it's important to have some fun with them.

After all, a fantasy football league with a girl commissioner just crowned a champion composed of a girl and an old fart while several other teams composed of macho humiliated guys scrambled to make sense of their failed genius.

I just have to figure out a way to keep Jen on my team next year.

You GO Girl!

Just A Thought

The Rhthym of Sport

Let's review now; I did not go to college and have absolutely no allegiance to any particular institution of higher learning. I have no caps, sweatshirts or bumper stickers proclaiming such allegiance. I am possibly the only man who will say – and quite frankly, I might add – that for me, New Years Day is watching the Rose Parade and then finding something to do away from my TV.

Simply put, when the debate comes up about the BCS Bowl issues, I am one fellow who certainly has no dogs in this race.

I could care less about it, which of course makes me the perfect writer to rise to the occasion and solve this whole mess for you.

We have this thing called college football that begins before the kids start back to school for the most part.

Everybody loves college football and certainly there is a whole lot of money to be made for these colleges every Saturday afternoon during the season.

They play about 12 games and the idea is to not only win

all 12 games, but to impress the computer geeks enough to warrant an invitation to the big championship game.

Sounds perfectly fair, but of course the marketing maggots that sleep with the college presidents of these fine institutions control this system and have making money as their sole priority which is totally fair because that is no different from practically anything else we do in life, so it's all good.

The schools make lots of money and the marketing maggots make even more money and so they sleep together happily ever after.

It's quite a nice system, really.

Many people – like EVERYONE outside the college presidents and marketing maggots – think this system stinks and want to see a true playoff system so the champion can be decided on an actual football field.

It's not a novel idea as every other college sport has a playoff system that narrows the field of teams down until they have their champion.

But the powers that be state that they simply can not have this playoff system because these gridiron boys have a serious obligation to study hard and do well on their finals and we must not distract them.

And the fact that the stories of college athletes graduating with a diploma that they can not read only evolves from this beloved game of FOOTBALL and no other college sport – EVER– is simply not a fair argument and you just need to let that go.

The system will never change because our beloved college

presidents and their sleeping marketing buddies are passionately dedicated to preserving the educational superiority of the college football player over all other college athletes.

I know…. I thought the same thing…. The irony drips from all this logic.

But here's a point I'm thinking nobody cares about.

Anybody who plays sports knows that a game – be it football, baseball, hockey, whatever – is won and lost by the rhythm of the game.

Team sports are made up of several well tuned athletes working together as one unit in a highly charged competitive environment to reach one goal.

You get into a rhythm, a groove, a focused cadence that gets all these wonderful parts working together like a seamless sculpture that you hope well take the team right up to the championship game.

In college football, they give you five or six weeks off after the season before you play in whatever bowl game these computer geeks have invited you to.

And it's getting worse – they now have about 4-5 bowl games AFTER New Years Day!

And we wonder why the games end up mostly being awful examples of what the teams did in November?

You tell me how a team keeps their rhythm for a stagnant five weeks while they take those finals that prepares them not to be able to read their diplomas.

Please!

Most college students I know have their finals the week or so after Thanksgiving and then they're off for Christmas break.

Is the system fair?

Of course not, but not because of the computer geeks who send out the invitations.

It's not fair to the college football players who work so hard and then are asked to play the biggest game of their college career after taking six weeks off to cool off and break down their rhythm.

That's not fair.

Again, I don't even care much for college football, but the rhythm issue is a big reason.

I have no attraction to basketball, but I certainly enjoy March Madness. It's a couple of weeks – right at the end of their season – of energetic, sustained rhythm that cultivates into an exciting final outcome.

You'll never see that in college football.

But I did enjoy the Rose Parade.

Just A Thought

Intermission

I know you are frustrated because you can't put this book
down.
It's 100 of my favorite columns put in no particular order
So there really is no PartI/ PartII to speak of.
But in order to "look" professional – and give you a break
I'm giving you an intermission!
So take a break, get a fresh cup of coffee
Then come back and enjoy the rest of the stories!
You're Welcome

Those Poor Wealthy

It is true that I am the one who said, "The person who said money isn't everything had too damn much of it to be saying such a thing!"

I am also the one who said, "You shouldn't let money control your life".

But the reality is that the more money you have, the more fun you can have on this glorious planet we call home. Though I often say that I never let money control my life, I understand that it does, in fact, control my life – and a lot I might add.

I'm in the best financial state of my life right now and I'm still living paycheck to paycheck. I'm a car repair away from financial disaster. I always have lots of vacation time to burn at the end of the year because, as much as I'd love to travel, my company does not pay me extra so I can travel the world and stay in hotels, rent cars and play in the worlds best playgrounds – and still pay my rent, electricity and cable service.

It's not the best life, but I'm not complaining.

Like I say, I'm in the best shape I've ever been financially. I pay my bills every month and have just enough left over to have a few small treats to keep me happy.

I mention all this because I was thinking the other day – which always leads to trouble – about those who do not struggle.

The wealthy.

I went to a brunch a week ago at a very nice home in the very high rent district of the city. These people's idea of a recession is when the maid calls in sick and they actually have to walk out to the mailbox and get their own mail – oh, the shame of it!

Their home is perfectly manicured with everything in its place and there is nothing that reflects a Wal Mart price tag, that's for sure.

Don't get me wrong, these were very nice people.

But it struck me that their garden was well manicured – but they have a service come do that.

Their home was pristine and very orderly – but they have a maid and butler who take care of that.

The food was great – but they had a catering service come to do that.

I'm guessing they just had to get out of bed and change – and they didn't have to make their bed!

It was a nice party and it certainly was nice of them to open their home and provide such a lovely atmosphere for the occasion.

But as I left, I didn't feel envy for them, I felt sorry for them.

They never feel that sheer joy of walking out your door with twenty bucks in your pocket, knowing all the bills are paid and the twenty bucks is yours to party with tonight!

They never know the absolute comfort of climbing into your bed with fresh sheets after wrestling all morning with that damn skirt thing around the base while you're trying to change your sheets.

They don't know the orgasmic flavor explosion on those rare occasions when you can sit down with a special meal brought to you by a daring impulse at the supermarket which is very naughty but the payoff is so rewarding (there is nothing like all beef hot dogs, my friend, nothing like it, indeed!).

The wealthy of the world never get to experience these wonderful emotions of little luxuries.

These emotional moments, though small and simple, bring so much hope, joy and a sense of value to people like me.

I truly can feel like the king of the world by simply crawling into my old worn-out bed with fresh sheets.

I've never been sworn to poverty, though my skills apparently were.

I fully understand that the more money you have in your pocket when you walk out that door, the more fun you can have.

And I'm a guy who really wants to have a lot of fun.

But not everything is what it appears to be.

I feel for those wealthy people who go through life never having the chance to sit down with an all beef hot dog dinner and feeling that orgasmic explosion of flavorful luxury with every bite!

Somehow I just think they miss so much of life's real adventures.

Just A Thought

Turning Up 40

So I thought I would spend some time talking to you about a milestone that I have recently achieved.

I just turned forty.

Actually I didn't really see this as being that big of a deal. If you stay reasonably within the boundaries of basic living, with a little luck, everyone will hit the big four-ooooooohhhhhh sometime during their travels through this wonderful experience called life.

I worked at the morgue (creative writers do things like that) for about a year and a half, and I can assure you that the alternative to turning forty is not a very pleasant one, indeed.

I am more than happy to turn the page of my calendar and start down the road of yet another minutes to hours, hours to days, days to weeks, and weeks into still another year gone by.

Some people really get emotional about turning forty.

Some get so depressed that you'd swear that their favorite college team had been put on probation and will not be allowed to play in this year's Boredom Bowl.

It's a rather grim way to start a decade, if you ask me.

They say that women take forty harder than men, but I'm not so sure.

True, it is not much fun keeping company with a woman who thinks she's getting old, but how many men have you seen turn forty and go out to get a tattoo, pierce their ears, or buy that motorcycle they've always wanted?

Or even worse, find those young babes attractive and think they have a shot'?

At forty, women get down in the dumps.

Men get down in the gutter.

But really now, most of us don't really have a problem with getting older. Most of us are grateful to be alive and look forward to making the most of every opportunity that comes their way in the next forty years.

I do see signs of getting older though.

I went to a Beach Boys concert for my birthday. No other group brings back my youth like the Beach Boys. What a shock it was to look through my binoculars only to find gray hairs, sagging chins, bald heads, wrinkles and droopy eyes. "My God, they're Old Men!!!…. IMPOSTERS!!!" I screamed.

The thought of my Beach Boys as being mortal was a major shock to this old beachcomber's heart.

I aged twenty years that night alone.

I don't have to squint any more to find gray hair on my head, and my hair is much easier to part down the middle now than before.

I don't mind, though.

If the hair goes gray, fine. If it just goes, that's fine, too.

I never saw my hair as being a major part of my existence – except during those flower-powered '60s days of my youth.

I was soooooo cool, then.

I still remember everything about my youth… whether it happened or not.

I know all the answers to life, though no one ever stops to ask me.

Certainly, I enjoy looking at all the attractive young ladies, but I am blessed with enough horse-sense to know better than try and make a fool of myself by thinking they might find me attractive without a sports car and fancy portfolio.

Parties, large get-togethers and social events are now avoided when possible.

The children now tuck me in at night.

I no longer have any patients with people who don't think and act the same as me.

Especially when behind the wheel of my car.

I see all these 'beautiful people' strutting around the health club and want to throw up.

I'm in heaven when the girls are all out for the evening and I can sit back in the peace and quiet of a good book.

I see people with young children and thank my stars that my girls are old enough to forget my name.

I don't like sleeping in.

There is no better way to start the day than to get up early and sit out on the porch with the sports page and a cup of coffee.

Athletes that are my age are considered antiques in their sport.

I like a vacation that isn't busy.

Sitting around a lake chatting with family and friends is just fine with me, thank you.

But I guess the bottom line is that age is really a state of mind.

I don't think of myself as forty...I'm sixteen with twenty-four years of experience.

For my birthday, I read a book about one of my favorite people...Jack Benny.

Now here's a guy who was thirty-nine for many, many years.

That's the right attitude.

So I've reached this great milestone in life...I'm forty.

But it's not how many times that you turn the calendar of life that counts.

It's how you fill it in.

Just A Thought

Who's Passing the Torch

Remember when JFK was President?

He was the one who got us all motivated towards physical fitness.

He's the one who started the President's Council on Physical Fitness.

Remember how we had to take all those tests in school in order to get a grade in P.E.?

We had to do sit ups, chin ups, push ups, the 50 yard dash.

Everyone participated.

It was as much a part of school as was book reports, math exams and crushes on cheerleaders.

JFK was our leader and he showed us how to spend our free time.

We all still have vivid memories of the Kennedys out in a sailboat, running along the beaches or playing tag football in their back yard.

We fell in love with the Kennedy lifestyle and for the first time, we as a nation, began to look at physical fitness as an important part of our daily lives and not just something reserved for the athletes.

Today that same commitment towards keeping in shape remains an important part of our generation. Even though our lives have changed a great deal from those early days in the 60s, you can still see a great number of adults outside walking, running or working out in gyms.

Today's parents are very busy people.

Both the husband and wife need to bring home the bacon.

There's a lot more pressure on today's parents to keep up with the Jones.

Life is not as relaxed as it used to be, yet we still seem just as committed to keeping in shape as ever before.

But there's something that really bothers me.

While the parents are out walking and running, I can only ask, "Where's the kids?"

The sad truth is for the most part, the kids are at home sitting in front of their big screens playing video games, eating chips and drinking colas.

One of the saddest reports I've seen is the one that says that today's kids may be the first generation to reverse the trend and actually lower the life expectancy in our country.

Many doctors say that if families make no changes in their lifestyles, many of today's children will be headed on a course that will see heart attaches before the age of 50 as a common occurrence.

And the problem is not just with the parents.

Most children have physical fitness two times a week and all too often, these times are spent just playing games.

Many high school kids have P.E. as an elective!

Most elementary school children couldn't tell you a chin-up from a pushup.

The days of taking physical fitness tests for grades are long gone.

The schools have gone back to letting physical fitness be reserved for the athletes only.

They come home from school with virtually no physical fitness.

Their diets are horrendous.

And they spend entirely too much time sitting in front of their video games.

How sad it is to think that many of today's parents will outlive their children.

We can't wait for another Kennedy to come forward and show us the way.

As parents, we need to take more responsibility for our family's well-being.

We need to take more control of our children's lives.

This is not to suggest that you throw away the video games and feed them nothing but spinach. But we can do so much better than we currently are.

Parents need to set an example to their children.

Many of them already do with all their activities that they are involved with, but they need to involve their children as well.

Why not take them out to the track with you when you go walking?

Encourage them to get out and get involved with some form of physical activity.

And where are the parents when it comes to talking about budgets within our schools.

We should have never permitted our schools to cut out the arts and physical fitness from our children's experience in education.

We've done well as adults in keeping ourselves in shape as our years increase, but we've done poorly as parents in passing on the torch of positive living to our children.

I can't help but think that JFK would be so disappointed if he were still around today.

Just A Thought

Rules We Have Created

Sorry to disturb you God, but we have a few items we need you to look at.

What do you have fellas?

Well sir, we have a baseball game down on Earth where a pitcher has taken a no-hitter into the eighth inning.

I know ... I've been watching it ... Red Sox and Yanks ... that kid's pitching a gem and I'm thinking he's gonna pull it off!

Unfortunately sir, we have information of a teammate was sitting next to him and talking to him after the sixth inning, so by rule, we have to break up the no-hitter.

[God looks bewildered] That's a rule?

Well sir, it actually falls under the superstitions market, but they really believe in this stuff.

Maybe he was just asking about his wife or something.

Doesn't matter, sir. They say if a team mate sits next to a pitcher and talks to him after the 5th inning of a no-hitter, the no-hitter gets broken up.

[God shakes his head] That's the rule?

Yes sir

[God looks frustrated] I was looking forward to the kid closing it out, too . Well do what you have to do .... anything else for me fellas?

Yes sir ... Ed McMann passed away this morning.

Oh .... ok .... Well he hasn't been well lately, and he's not that young any more I suppose. Any problems?

Yes sir... being that he's a celebrity, we have to schedule two more celebrities to come home.

[God looks at them confused] Excuse me.

Well it's another one from the superstitions market that celebrities always die in threes. And now they've added the three S's.

The three S's?

Yes sir ... senior, sick and sudden ... Ed qualifies as the senior, so now we have to bring home a celebrity who is sick and one whose death is sudden.

You are kidding, right? .... This isn't how they work down there?

Yes sir ... more superstition than rule, really, but they really believe in this stuff.

[God shakes his head in disbelief] Any suggestions?

Well sir, Farrah Fawcett has been battling cancer for some time and it would be fairly easy to just bring her home.

Yes, she has put up a good fight that's for sure ... I suppose she's earned her peace now and if it fits their silly rules, I don't have any problem bringing her home.

Yes sir …. so that's a senior and a sick … we just need a sudden.

Well they have created so many ways to die suddenly, I wouldn't think that would be a big problem .

[God pauses]

You know, here's an idea … I snuck into the Staple Center last night to watch this kid Jackson rehearse for his upcoming tour, and from what I saw, we might be doing more for his career by bringing him home now before that tour gets started.

Well sir, we certainly could create an accident.

He looks so fragile …. and you know he has never been good with his diets and medications… I don't think it's a stretch to see that one coming.

Yes sir, that would be easy to arrange.

[God shakes his head again] Too bad …I just love to watch that kid dance.

Well sir, once he comes to this side, he'll be good as new and you can watch him dance all you want.

[God brightens] Yeah …. be sure and schedule him to come see me as soon as he gets in …. I've been trying to get that moon walk step down for years and haven't even come close.

[God pauses in great enthusiasm] … Well, there you have it fellas …. this should cover their silly superstitions for now … anything else?

Yes sir …. Once we bring Michael home, we have to have a celebrity get pregnant.

[God looks at them dumbfounded] Excuse me?

Well sir, they say that celebrities die in 3s and that there needs to be a celebrity getting pregnant before another celebrity dies or that celebrity becomes number 4 instead of the start of another threesome.

[God looks at them with a pained expression] Remind me again, fellas …. this is the best species we have on this planet?

[In the background there is a crack of the bat and the announcer can be heard …. 'Oh, that's going to break up the no-hitter folks … and the rookie third baseman is kicking the dirt in disgust as he now understands you can't sit and talk to the pitcher after the 5th inning when he's pitching a no-hitter… oh, that's a shame …. the young pitcher was looking so strong too']

God hangs his head and shakes it in disbelief.

Just A Thought

Scanning the Universe

I write a lot of different things. Books, songs, articles, letters – wherever the creative juices lead me.

One form of writing I enjoy is plays.

The nice thing about plays is that it challenges you to be more visual and attentive to setting and dialog.

When you write a book or song, you permit the reader and listener to create their own visuals as they wish – it ain't your problem.

But in a play, you have to create the visual as well as a strong dialog to keep people from squirming in their seats and running for the exits.

The problem with writing a play is in the formatting.

You can spend an entire afternoon just setting up the tabs on your typewriter before you actually set out to create the story. It can be a pain, especially when someone borrows your typewriter and screws up all the tab settings in five minutes.

So you'd think that in this new world of modern technology the chore of writing a play would become a very simple task. Certainly, they have software you can buy for $200.00 that has everything neatly formatted for you, and as soon as I make two hundred bucks in my life, I'm all over that purchase, you can be sure.

For now I fumble in a cyber world that has trouble recognizing what I'm trying to do.

I wrote plays BEFORE God gave us the computer and the good people who created these wonderful machines had no idea that this world would have any appeal to playwrights.

Who knew?

Let me explain.

When I bought my brand spanking new computer with the works, I instinctively knew that I would likely want to put my plays that I wrote in the typewriter stone age on this new wonderful machine so I could access them whenever I wanted.

Writers are always going back to rewrite and tweak their old stuff.

So being the sharp customer that I am, I went all out and bought a scanner on the very same day!

This would enable me to simply scan my plays into my new computer as I wished.

Simple, right?

When I get my new toys all set up, I scan page one into my $50.00 scanner and this long skinny light slowly crawls over my page and pops up what it sees – page one of my play!

It asks me A) is this what you're scanning, Pops?

and B) where do you want us to throw this puppy?

I tell the scanner it looks good, go ahead and slap that bad boy into my computer in the folder I have already designated.

When my $50.00 scanner is done, I go to my $2,000.00 computer and pull up page one of my play.

What I'm looking at seems to be some form of cyber-lava lamp technology, because the words are all there, but they seem to float all over the page in no particular order.

No tabs.

No structure.

No order.

Just a page full of words – albeit the right words, I'll give it that.

When I bring this to the attention of a Techie person, they scoff at me that my computer program just didn't recognize it.

'So you're saying my $2,000.00 computer didn't recognize a sheet of paper that my $50.00 scanner clearly understood?'

Tech people are sensitive and usually end every conversation with rolling eyes and a 'you-just-don't-understand' exit.

I think I do understand – computers are – technically speaking – stupid!

The lesson here I suppose, is that computers are very much like our government.

We are well endowed with departments that clearly meets the needs of all people.

The problem is that one department has no idea what the other department is trying to do.

I'm thinking that computers really don't like scanners.

A $50.00 scanner can do something a $2,000.00 computer can't do – recognize my old play.

Why should a computer cooperate with a scanner, really?

'Yea, here's the crap your cheap scanner just threw at me – hey, pal, why don't you dump that and use my new programs to write a new play, huh, fella? Common!?!'

One of the most contradictive phrases in our world is 'smart computers'.

There is no such thing as long as we have $50.00 scanners that can show any of these slick techie machines up.

But for now, I'm thinking that until I hit the mother load and grab me a $200.00 payday, I'm going to stick to writing books, songs and articles.

Just a Thought

Stand Up Already

Remember the 'Leave it to Beaver' era?

Oh, those were the good old days, right?

Tranquil, gentle and no conflicts.

Everyone just went about their business.

Everyone had their role.

Everyone fit into their neat little boxes without complaint.

How we long for those days and there are some from that generation who would argue that the world has gone to hell since the sixties.

Being that I am a member in good standing of the generation that brought you the sixties, I will go out on a limb and say that not only did we need the sixties then, but we are closing in on needing another sixties today.

The fifties were very vanilla.

The women stayed home and had dinner ready for their husbands when they got home.

The children were never aloud to challenge authority at any time.

The blacks paid their bus fare and quietly went to the back of the bus.

And our government went about their business without being challenged by we, the people who put them in office.

Perfect.

We were a neatly packaged, fall in line society of people who simply conformed to what we were told.

When the sixties came around, we started thinking about it.

The more we thought about it, the more we started to challenge it.

The more we challenged it, the more people started to realize that a society that merely conforms is not a society at all.

Without the women helping out, we would have never won WWII. Why should they be left in the kitchen if they have other dreams and talents to offer our community?

If a black person pays his fee to ride the bus, why should he or she be told where they have to sit?

And when our politicians tell us one thing about a war and two months later do the absolute opposite as our brothers are coming home in body bags, why shouldn't we stand up and shake up the system a little.

I am proud of what we did in the sixties and I feel strongly that even though it got ugly, we were absolutely correct to break this country out of its vanilla lifestyle and give people the hope that if they have a dream and are willing to put in the work, they can achieve their dreams no matter who they are or what color they are.

That's the America we fought for!

The sixties made our country a much better country.

Put that in your banana peel and smoke it.

A whole generation stood up and said, 'stop it with all this nonsense'.

It was painful.

It got ugly often.

We didn't do a perfect job, but we stood strong and refused to conform to the Leave it to Beaver mentality.

And because we did, our country became a much stronger, diverse and creative country.

A country for ALL the people.

I see the pot boiling again today.

We are all getting angry and we are making the mistake of thinking if we vote for the 'other' candidates, it will solve our problems.

We got mad at Bush and those Republicans, so we voted them out and put in the Democrats.

Now we're mad at the Democrats so we are going to throw them all out and put in the Republicans.

And in two years – I Guarantee it!- we will be pissed off at EVERYONE and vote for ANYONE who says they are not a politician.

And two years after that …

How many elections will it take before we, the people, realize that we are channeling our anger at the wrong thing?

It's not about Republicans or Democrats; it's about the system we have created.

The rules for elections have been created by people who need to win the next election.

Control is in the hands of advertising agencies and political action groups who have come to understand that far too many of us live with this notion that it is our patriotic duty to vote every election, and though we piss and moan about how negative the campaigns are, we still go out and vote saying at least that one is the lesser of two evils.

As long as we hold that mentality, those ad agencies will only be motivated to spend more money smearing the opponent instead of giving any solutions to the worlds problems.

They get paid handsomely to win elections and as long as we enable them by insisting that we are willing to vote for the lesser of two evils, they will continue to spend millions on hateful, mean ads.

You brought it on by not standing up and saying NO- We Do NOT Approve Of This Message!

Let's save this country before it's too late.

Just A Thought

Thanks To The Baseball Gods

I grew up in San Diego. I spent my youth surfing, going to school, playing baseball and surfing again.

Baseball was the passion in my youthful heart.

My baseball history was loving the Padres and hating the Dodgers.

Certainly, any real fan of the game would not be impressed with my baseball heritage.

But I loved the game.

I would spend each February at the breakfast table asking my daughters why this particular day was the most important day of the year. As they grew older, they learned to respond correctly, 'Pitchers and Catchers report to spring training – pass me the juice, huh, dad?'

The crack of the bat.

The smack of the Mitt.

The smell of grass, peanuts and beer.

Take me out to the ball game – clearly the greatest song ever written.

No clocks, cheerleaders or halftime entertainment.

Baseball.

Played the way baseball should be played and knowing why it should be played that way.

Sometimes the baseball Gods just seem to smile on us.

We get the opportunity to witness something special that we know only comes every now and then.

We come to understand different eras and how wrong it is to compare one against the other.

I appreciate my era as much as my Dad appreciated his.

That's baseball.

It's a love affair like no other.

This year, we were able to see something so very special for a baseball fan that really defies any allegiance we may have.

Something so special that regardless of your personal preferences it made you simply sit back and take the moment in for all that it was.

You didn't root as much as you simply admired what was evolving in front of you.

The Boston Red Sox won the World Series.

Yes, you read that correctly, even though my 'smart' computer showered the comment with red lines, it is spelled correctly and confirmed:

The Red Sox have won the World Series!

But it's not simply that the Red Sox won, it's more how they won that makes you speechless.

Down three games to none against their hated rival Yankees in the ALCS, the Red Sox found themselves a few outs away from yet another winter of futility.

Then the baseball Gods smiled and decided to give baseball fans a real treat.

The Sox came back against the better Yanks and beat them four straight to gain a World Series birth.

Then they came up against a better Cardinal team and beat them four straight to give me and so many others the opportunity to say something no one has said since 1918.

The Boston Red Sox won the World Series.

They didn't have the better team.

They didn't have the smoothest game.

But they clearly played like a team that didn't have a curse, that's for sure.

Even the Babe had to be smiling after this one.

And how fitting it was that they won it in Saint Louis.

Cardinal fans are noted as the best fans in baseball.

I don't agree with that.

I like the Boston, New York and Philly fans. They yell and scream at you with a passion and intensity that can only be appreciated when you're a laid-back southern Californian.

But the Cardinal fans are great.

They know the game and they appreciate the history.

Boy did they get the history this time.

And though their beloved Cards were the victims, I am certain that the Cardinal fans understood the history and have nothing but good things to say.

They didn't see their Cardinals lose the Series, they only saw what the rest of us saw.

They saw the Boston Red Sox win the Series.

So we now will have to find another curse.

We will have to find another Bridesmaid.

We will have to find another baseball story of dreams so close but never fulfilled.

The Boston Red Sox have truly won the World Series.

As a baseball fan, this is going to be a very warm winter, indeed.

The Boston Red Sox won the World Series.

What will the baseball Gods think of next?

Just A Thought

Proms and SuperBowls

As a father surrounded by women, I will be the first to admit that when it comes to senior proms, we men are simply clueless.

Whether you are talking about my senior prom or my daughters several presidents later, the male race simply doesn't get it.

It's far too much hype, too much anxiety and frankly, much to do over something as silly as a dance.

We men just don't understand that kind of hype, really.

Now I know that you women have the perfect retort by boldly standing up to that pompous male comment, looking us straight in the eye and saying two simple words.

Super Bowl.

Case closed, it's a draw!

Back to the business at hand.

First there's the dress code. For the guys, they rent a tux. They can choose from a few colors, and for those with a little personality, wear red tennis shoes, but for the most part, a tux is a tux. You not only don't worry about other guys wearing the same tux, you actually expect it.

The ladies on the other hand start shopping for their prom dress during summer vacation. It must be fashionable and in step with today's moods, yet you must be certain that no other young lady shows up in the same dress. This is why young ladies always go shopping in packs.

And of course, a father will never understand the value of spending $200 on a dress that she wouldn't dare be caught wearing any time after the prom.

"Hey, isn't that the dress you wore to the prom?" is as devastating as zits before a date, bad hair days, pop quizzes in math and the break up of the Beach Boys.

Actually I just threw in that last one in a humble attempt at relating to these things.

A prom dress is a one-time expenditure. No discussion required.

Now on prom day, the guy picks up his tux, takes a shower about an hour before he needs to pick up his date and swings by the florist on the way to pick up the flowers.

He has plenty of time to go to the gym and pick up a few games of basketball during the day.

The ladies start prom day before the sun does.

There is an agenda of things to do that men will never understand.

This agenda will build to a frantic state of panic by four o'clock when her date is due to pick her up.

I will make no attempt at explaining any of this. I have no

idea why, on this one day, doing nails, hair, make-up and getting dressed should be a ten hour
episode of intensified anxiety.

I just found a baseball game on the tv and waited for my calling;

"Daddy, you have to run to the store and pick up…"

Which began two innings into the game and reoccurred every ten minutes upon my return.

Three roles of film later, the elegant couple is finally off to their dance.

There is a calm in the house that is quite soothing to a father who has spent the day trying to navigate through the anxiety that this most special day of your entire life has prompted.

The real interesting part of all this comes the day after.

With everyone clamoring to hear all the wonderful details of the glorious prom night, the response from your senior becomes the same response that seniors will have throughout every generation.

"Oh it was okay."

After months of preparations, months of anguish over what color to paint your nails, transportation, flowers, where to eat and all, it comes to an unconvincing shrug of the shoulders, "Oh it was okay."?

The truth is that the senior prom, in all its hype and anticipation, is merely a dance.

Few of the boys will sweat the starch out of their tux on the dance floor.

The young ladies are more interested in checking out all the dresses, hair- dos, nails and flowers than they are getting those starchy-stiff guys out on the dance floor.

My daughter spent about thirty seconds talking about the prom and the rest of the weekend talking about the after-prom.

I smiled as I realized that some things never change.

I barely remember my senior prom, but boy I could tell you stories about the great party we all had after the prom.

I knew exactly what my daughter was talking about, which for a father with teenagers, is a very celebrated occasion.

We are funny animals.

We spend months talking and hyping the prom with all its elegance, pageantry and magic, but when it's all over, we would rather talk about the pizza, jeans and T- shirts of the after-prom.

No matter what generation you call your own, the prom story always reads the same.

It's funny, isn't it?

In all fairness to the ladies, I could have just as easily written this column the day after the Super Bowl.

Just A Thought

Rethinking Fitness

I understand that I am a retired old man now. I also understand and appreciate people younger than I staying so focused on physical fitness with their latest gadgets, must wear attire and power drinks. I was young once too and well remember that when it comes to relationships of a human nature, judging a book by it's cover absolutely counts.

With humans, our attraction to one another pretty much begins with a visual profiling.

The rest of the animal kingdom all have the same book cover. You never hear momma Lion say, "Look at that stud over there ... I like the head of hair he's got going" .... Grrrrrrrr.

That's why God designed the other animals to just have a particular time of year for females to go into heat and let the studly fellas fight over who gets to be the dad.

It's not a very romantic world for sure, and it is a big point of reference in any discussion of why humans are better than the rest of the animals on our planet.

Animals mate once a year to carry on the species, while

humans have sex to connect with those we love every season for love and affection …. and lust …. not for babies necessarily, and it appears that it's the males who are in a constant state of heat.

The book cover matters to us, not to Lions, Tigers and Bears.

Which brings me to my topic today, which actually has nothing to do with animals, making babies or the big question: Why did God design the females to go into heat at a specific time of year in all the other animals while designing human males to be in perpetual heat all the time with us?

I'm guessing that people who think God doesn't have a sense of humor have not been very observant.

Obviously, my topic today deals with the human spirit.

I like to take walks.

When I lived downtown, I just loved heading out on a nice day to explore all the wonderful sights and sounds of the city I love.

When I moved out of the city, I found a great little park with lots of nature trails that go around a small lake and can accommodate those who wish to be challenged as well as those who wish to stroll.

I try to get out there at least once a week.

They don't allow runners.

They don't allow bikes.

It's nature and the trails are for walking.

The more I go over to this lake, the more troubled I become.

The 'easy' trail goes about a mile and a half around the lake with plenty of photo opts for turtles, cranes, and deer as well as a quiet, still lake.

There are no boats.

No fishing.

In fact they have many signs to let you know that you are to stay on the trail and not wander off to disrupt the echo system of nature.

And they are serious about their rules.

You get the picture – this is a place to get away from the world and become one with the natural nature we so often loose touch with.

Yet every time I go, there are always many neighbors hitting these trails at a brisk pace with their earplugs dialed into their motivational music, wristbands they constantly check to verify proper heart rates, calories burned and whatnot and wearing the latest attire that proclaims them to be serious about their health.

As I stroll around the lake, I've lost count of how many turtles I've seen basking in the sunlight on a branch by the shore.

My seriously healthy walkers have probably not seen one.

I've stopped to listen to the cranes taking off or the call of a distant bird, while my neighbors have listened to their favorite recording star.

Again, I am not against people working out and taking their health serious.

I fully admit that at my age, it wouldn't hurt me to take my health a little more serious as well.

But here's an idea: How about once a week leaving all that trendy gear at home, slap on some shorts and a tee shirt and STROLL around the lake and see how many turtles you can find.

The rest of the week is yours to do as you will, but for just one day, how about working on your soul.

Earplugs were created for asphalt, not trails

Stress is the leading cause of heart disease and these trails are the perfect medicine for the stressful loads we carry every day in this crazy world we call life.

After all, your book can have a great cover, but its true value will always be the story created inside.

One day of the week you can work on the story inside.

It can – and should be – a great story.

Just A Thought

Leave'm Alone, Already

Let me start out be saying that I am very much of an animal lover.

I will be the first in line for any cause that fights for the preservation of our national wildlife community.

There are few things that I enjoy more than to sit back and enjoy a nature show on NatGeo.

To watch the graceful Eagle in flight with the deep blue sky as a backdrop and the majestic mountains and valleys as its playground.

Or the powerful Grizzly Bear playfully slapping and bouncing along the stream in search of his 'catch of the day'.

The animal kingdom is the greatest source of fellowship the good Lord could have provided us, and I believe that we all have an obligation and responsibility to do all we can to insure that every member of the animal world has the opportunity to live and grow within their natural environment that they were created for.

Although I am happy to see so many people working towards building a better world for our animals, I've got to be honest and tell you that I am becoming very concerned about our methods.

We're a funny group, we humans.

We seldom let well enough alone.

The simple solution is rarely our cup of tea.

We love our world of gadgets and toys.

We invent new methods of doing something and, instead of letting it go at that, we rush back to the lab to invent something that is more powerful, more efficient and more durable.

Our good scientists who are dedicated to preserving our animals have done very well keeping many of our animal friends from becoming faint memories.

But I can't help but think that they have gone a bit too far with all this research stuff.

They put the animal to sleep, weigh him, measure everything on him, draw tubes of blood from him, yank out one of his teeth, (they tell us that this tooth will tell them a lot about this animal), staple an identification tag on his ear and place a large, brightly colored collar around his neck to transmit radio signals.

After all this, the compassionate scientist will softly gaze into the camera and tell us that this procedure 'doesn't bother the animal at all!'

Now who do they think they are kidding?!

The dentist will always smile and tell us that we won't feel a thing... until we are far removed from the dentists office and the Novocain wares off.

Here this poor animal was enjoying a nice day amongst his own when he suddenly feels a sharp pain in his shoulder, then is chased around by this huge metal bird with blowing wings until he becomes so dizzy and weak he cannot stand on his own feet. He crumbles to the ground, fighting to regain his strength before he losses the battle and fades off.

When he comes to, he finds his peers have left him, he realizes that his ear, shoulder and rump are quite sore, his head feels like someone took a baseball bat to it and he has this contraption around his neck that makes him most uncomfortable.

Yet we are to believe that all of this testing stuff has no affect on the animal's lifestyle.

I don't know, I think animals did very well for thousands of years without our helpful gadgets and radio waves.

I mean, if we let this go on, our forests, jungles and oceans will be jam-packed with radio signals from creatures large and small and the peaceful, gentle colors of mother nature will be cluttered with bright, florescent neckbands that will do as much to helping the hunters as it will our scientist who are so dedicated to preserving them.

Don't get me wrong, I truly do appreciate the efforts that are being made towards understanding and preserving our animal neighbors.

But I can't help but think that if we really want to help the animal kingdom, we should leave them alone and stop messing up their environment.

After all, most of these documentaries too often tell us that an animal's only true enemy is man.

The Elephant and the Rhino are almost extent, yet these animals have no natural enemies within the animal kingdom.

Only man has caused their demise and what is so sad is that we have killed them not for our own survival, but for sport, jewelry and some pretty purses.

I think we need to get a grip on all these gadgets and radio trinkets that we keep slapping on these poor animals. If we really are sincere about helping the animal kingdom survive, we need to stop killing them for our own selfish reasons and put our efforts into protecting the environment that we all, animals as well as humans, must exist within.

It really doesn't bother them?

Please

Just A Thought

Missing the Trains

It's common knowledge that the best sight is hind sight.

We can always get a clearer picture of an event when we look back on it.

Whether we are reading history books or looking back on our own life, the past is full of moments that generate a shoulda response.

They shoulda gone that direction.

I shoulda made that choice.

God shoulda thrown another meteor at us and started all over again at that time.

We love looking back because we are all geniuses when we do.

I'm an absolute genius when talking about the 60s, which is somewhat ironic coming from a guy who in the 60s was a care-free teenager with more salt water on the brain than knowledge and whose name was never brought up in conversations about gifted programs.

Yet here I am now able to explain anything you need to know about the 60s in masterful articulation.

I am in awe of myself.

I enjoy reading books about history, especially our country's history.

I find it fascinating that you can read every book on the Revolutionary War and you will never come away with a clear explanation of how we won that war.

There is none.

We just won it, that's all we know.

But there will always be another professor who will write another book and we will all read it and come away with the same thought.

'There's no way we should have won that war ... they should have kicked our butts.'

That's the fun of hind sight.

I was thinking the other day about one part of history where I think we really dropped the ball.

Actually there are about a million places in history where we dropped the ball, but this story is not about my genius.

As I was sitting at a railroad crossing watching a very long train pass by, the thought occurred to me that our country really blew it when it comes to our railroad system.

Depending on where you live, the story varies a bit, but generally speaking our railroads have been reduced to simply moving goods from point A to point B – and we are not the goods being transported.

When planes got to a point where they could take on passengers, everybody wanted to fly. With a country this big, the thought of getting to another part of the country in a few hours was quite an exciting thing.

The more our air travel developed, the more our railroad system became reduced to transporting lumber and memories of how it use to be.

I remember how much fun it use to be to take the girls to the airport just to watch the planes take off and land. As a single parent, this was always a great activity that entertained the girls at no cost to the old man.

But the times, they are a changin'

The days where air travel and visiting airports were an exciting and enjoyable experience have been replaced by security checks, long lines and rude business people who think because they fly more often, they deserve more courtesies than you.

Simply put, flying the unfriendly skies today is a dreaded experience that I avoid unless I absolutely have to.

And I'm thinking I am not alone on this.

The sad news is that I often don't have any choice, which brings me back to the trains. My home town is San Diego and I live now in Nashville. If everyone is getting together at Moms, I have two choices.

I can deal with airports that have no customer service, filled with anxious, rude people so I can get on a four hour flight that comes with no customer service, filled with anxious, rude people and see Mom by supper time (and her always great home cooking).

Or I can jump in my car and drive for four days – with

another four days driving back and spend whatever time left on visiting the family.

Well nobody has that much time, so I really am left with no other choice but to put up with flying with a bunch of rude, anxious people.

What fun!

I wish we could have had better vision to see that when planes began taking people to all corners of our world, there would always be a need for an alternative travel experience.

In this post 9-11 era, I am certain that I am not alone in saying that given a choice, I'd much rather grab a train for a two day run to San Diego and avoid the horrible airport experience if I could.

Unfortunately that's a choice I don't have and there is little reason to think I ever will. There are ways of doing it, but the routes are very limited and frankly does nothing to encourage people like me to take the plunge.

Europe has kept train travel as a viable alternative to planes and they seem to be doing very nicely with it.

We certainly dropped the ball on the opportunity to keep railroad travel as an attractive alternative to air travel for those of us not so consumed by fast-paced lifestyles.

We shoulda known better.

All Aboard!

Just A Thought

My '41 Woody

So there I was in this art store picking up some goodies for a project I was working on for my daughter.

As I was browsing, I looked down a row that was bursting with models. Mostly cars and planes, with all the paints, glue, brushes and accessories needed to create a masterpiece.

As I walked past, I thought to myself, 'Gee, I sure loved to make model cars when I was a kid. Growing up sure ain't much fun.'

About two aisles past, I came to a frozen halt.

I cautiously looked around as if I was secretly seeking a face for the voice that had stopped me.

I quickly realized that the voice came from within.

That little voice in the basement of my conscious that always has great ideas that gets me in trouble.

You know, big fella, you do live alone.

The girls are out of the nest, you know.

It's not like you have to run off to track meets, soccer games or anything.

You don't have any significant other who would nag you and tell you how immature you are.

It wouldn't hurt to go back there and at least look at the models, would it?

I stood there for a minute looking around to see if anyone else was listening to this.

Then I got to thinking.

You know, it wouldn't hurt to just look.

After all, I'm in no particular hurry.

It might be fun to look at some of the models they put out today and see if they are anything like I use to get as a kid.

Feeling a bit sinful in my adventure, I did an about face and headed back towards the row of models assuring myself that if, by some remote chance, they had a '41 Woody, I just might snag it.

The '41 Woody was the ultimate surfer dudes dream car. Every surfer growing up on the sunny beaches of Southern California dreamed of one day owning a Woody. You would be the coolest of all surfer dudes if you could throw your board in the back of a Woody. The beach babes would be all over you. Way better than having a VW, the compromise of most dreaming surfers.

I snap myself back to reality.

After all, this is Nashville and I doubt they have a lot of calls for '41 Woodys around here.

As I turned down the row of models, I once again froze in my tracks.

With my jaw bouncing off the floor, I gaze at not one, but three boxes of '41 Woodys – complete with a SURFBOARD!

I was all over it.

It was CLEARLY a sign from God!

I bought the model, glue, paints, brushes, the whole works and headed home to pursue my childhood again.

For the next week I was in Heaven.

I meticulously painted each part and gave absolute attention to every detail. I even painted my surfboard the same as mine when I was younger and even dripped some wax from a candle on top to give it that surfer authenticity.

I simply can't remember having this much fun with a project.

When it was finished, I had a wonderful home set up for it on a shelf in my writing room.

It is totally awesome, dude!

You know, once you pass fifty years of age, you seem to come to a crossroad.

You can become a grumpy old fart who complains about the younger generation and how things were better in my days.

Or you can simply digress by letting that voice in the basement of your conscious have its' way with you.

Heck, I enjoyed building my Woody so much, I signed up with the co-ed softball team at my church.

Who knows, maybe this old age stuff could be some fun.

And yes, I didn't forget my project for my daughter.

It too turned out pretty good.

Just A Thought

High - Rising Crops

There has been a lot of doomsday talk going around lately that's got me wondering.

Life isn't what it use to be down on the farm.

For sale signs seem to be the biggest commodity coming out of our farmlands nowadays.

Turning the soil no longer turns the profit.

Being a big city boy, I am quite certain that I am not the person to talk about our agricultural needs.

But I am a creative dreamer, and creative dreamers are great for looking at a problem and seeing new opportunities and possibilities instead of hopeless miseries.

If the farms aren't working like they are, by God, let's not sell them…let's fix them!

It seems to me that one solution to our farming problems might be to start thinking upward instead of outward.

Why not build sky-scrapper farms?'

If a family grows tomatoes in 500 acres of farmland, why not build a 27-story high-rise on maybe five of those acres?

The farmer could grow just as many tomatoes on those stacked acres as he could on those 500 spread out acres.

Oh I know, I'm probably way off base here, but maybe not.

Our food would be grown indoors under perfect conditions.

They wouldn't have to spray all those cancer-causing chemicals to keep the bugs away.

Being that the food would be grown indoors, the farmer would not be at the mercy of mother nature.

Not only could we grow bigger and healthier produce, but we could grow them all year long.

There would no longer be such a thing as in-season!

Think about it!

Corn on the cob and fresh strawberry pie at Christmas?!?!

No problem!!

Droughts… floods… heat waves… freezes…would no longer have any impact on our food chain!

It seems to me that the farmer wouldn't lose anything. In fact, I would think that they would save money because they wouldn't have to buy all those chemicals or some of that equipment that they would if their farm was spread out over 500 acres.

Consumers would win, because prices would stay fairly stable, and a shopper could expect to find every fruit and vegetable at their produce store every day of the year- without a consequence for buying at the wrong time of the year.

Land, which is quickly becoming more valuable to us, would no longer be a major factor.

Hey, we could build a high-rise farm in the middle of Manhattan and even save a few bucks in shipping costs!

We could let nature and all it's critters have more land to play on.

I don't know, it makes since to me, albeit a big city boy who grew up on the beaches and knows very little about farming.

I'm sure there are many negatives about this, or someone else would have thought about it a long time ago.

But we live in a time of great challenges.

If we are to survive, we are going to have to start thinking more creatively for the solutions to our problems.

A high rise farm may seem a bit out in left field, but many of our great inventions came from left field.

Left field certainly isn't a bad place to look for the answers to many of today's problems.

High rise farming.

No chemicals needed.

Your favorite fruits and vegetables in season every day of the year.

People no longer arguing over space.

No more stories about mother nature wiping out our crops with droughts, floods, freezes or heat waves.

Sounds crazy, doesn't it?

Funny what ideas might come from a creative writer like

me, sitting on a brisk winter's evening dying to sink my teeth into a hot, crisp corn on the cob?

Just A Thought

[NOTE to reader- this was a column I wrote around 1992ish – it is now 2018 and high-rising farms are becoming a thing now. Books are selling like hot cakes and many high-rises are actually creating farms on their rooftops with more plans on the way…. You are all welcome!]

I'm Finally Cleared

For the past thirty years I've had a lot of trouble sleeping.

I have constantly fought off the urge to become a recluse and hide out like my old buddy Howard Hughes.

I felt like people kept looking at me and thinking, "That crazy Andy …. you know it could be HIM."

I have lived each and every day under an umbrella of suspicion.

Now it's over.

I can finally sleep at night knowing that the whole world once and for all knows without a doubt that Andy Smith is in FACT not Deep Throat!

I understood the connections that made some think that I was the guy.

I have never publicly attacked those who thought it was me.

I'm a compassionate, loving, forgiving kind a guy and I will not use my column to lash out at them or give any 'nannynanny-nanny-I-told-you-so!' commentaries.

Let the past go already, I'm ready to start a new chapter in my life.

Let the bygones be bygones, by golly.

It is once more great to be alive.

Now for those of you who have not known me that long, it all started when I wrote those letters to President Reagan.

The first one came after Mr Hollywood President decided to interrupt a Bugs Bunny special to hold a news conference. Now if Canada was invading Montana or something, I could understand that. But this news conference came at a time when there was ABSOLUTELY NOTHING going on in the whole wide world – except for the small detail of a really nice Bugs Bunny special that every parent bribed their kids to behave for if they wanted to watch it.

You can imagine the horror when I got my girls all excited for Bugs only to turn on the TV and find Elmer Thud with nothing to talk about.

I gave the President a piece of my mind about that one.

The second letter came when one of his staff said that most people in soup lines are only there for free food.

I couldn't believe my ears! Of course they're there for free food because they can't AFFORD to buy it with your Reaganomics, you idiot!

I wrote the Prez and again gave him an ear full on how any decent, sensitive President would clearly boot that SOB out of Washington for making such a lame, insensitive comment about the down and out of our country.

Ron never wrote me back of course, but I'm thinking that the FBI put me on the short list for Deep Throat after that.

How can you blame them.

After all, there are only a hand full of people who are crazy enough to sit down and actually write a letter to the President of the United States and call him an idiot.

I did it twice!

But that was ten years after Watergate.

You'd think the FBI would need a little more than a couple of letters to suspect me, now wouldn't ya?

Well, I have been consistant in my writings about money matters and have actually pointed out many times that to solve the problem of politics, follow the money.

And, of course I was a teenager in the '60s.

I did make a lot of un-charming remarks about the war we were in.

I did tell a draft counselor that there was no way I would EVER point a gun at someone else and end their life simply because they wore the wrong uniform (unless it was a Dodger uniform, but that's understood).

And I could be frequently found at those rock 'n roll concerts that gave a whole new meaning to the effects of second-hand smoke (that wasn't Camels they were smoking, my friends!).

I had trouble written all over me by the time I wrote those two letters.

The good people in the FBI knew full well that Andy Smith was someone to keep an eye on.

I'm sure I have a file with the FBI that is almost as frightening as my credit reports.

But alas, I'm clear.

I would have talked to Carl and Bob if they asked, but I've never been to Washington DC.

They'd have to meet me somewhere around Pacific Beach.

Yeah, under the old Crystal Pier would have made for nice drama, I'm thinking.

I could have easily given them as much as Deep Throat did.

Anyone who knows anything about American politics knows that if you're investigating the slime of politics, you only have to follow the money.

What surprises me from that era is that Bob and Carl actually needed to be told that?

They can't be that great of journalists if they needed that kind of information.

But that's not my problem any longer.

I'm free and clear of the whole incident and I'm back to living the American dream without concern.

Though, I'm guessing the FBI still keeps an eye on me.

For the record, I have never met Jimmy Hoffa.

Just A Thought

Everything is Beautiful

One of the more tragic days of my life came when I looked in the mirror and realized that I was not one of the beautiful people and would likely never be.

The Yuppie movement came and left before I ever had a chance to even put a down payment on a BMW.

The '80s were proclaimed the "ME" decade and this me didn't even have a prayer.

I was just never beautiful people material, I guess.

Sure, I could have gotten into one of those aerobic classes, but not with their dress codes.

All these florescent colored, skin tight outfits just don't cut it with me.

These people look like they spend more time getting ready for their workout than they do getting ready for work.

With every thread neatly in place, they strut into the aerobics room, and for the next forty minutes we hear a thunder of fast-paced rock 'n roll, pounding feet, clapping hands and various cat calls and howls of excitement.

When they exit, there are no signs of pain, every hair is still perfectly in place, and there is no sign of sweat penetrating from their cute little outfits.

I want an aerobics class where everyone wears baggy gray sweats.

And when the class is over, I want everyone to look like they just came out of a war zone.

I think people who don't experience pain and sweat should be charged double.

I guess I just don't have the right stuff to be beautiful people.

Beautiful people have a very specific set of rules that tells them what to say, what to wear and what to drive.

It's not enough to drink bottled water…it has to be a specific brand of bottled water.

It's not enough to eat out… you must be able to carry on a conversation about your favorite sushi.

Suits are nice, but if you want to be beautiful people, you simply must wear a "power" tie, whatever the hell that is.

In fact, everything you wear, from your suit to your underwear, must come with a specific tag of a specific brand name with a specifically higher price tag.

And who says cloning is still years away?

The beautiful people of the world all wear the same clothes…say the same thing…drive the same cars… and go to the same places.

While medical science debates the moral ethics of cloning, the beautiful people of the world have already perfected it…right under our noses.

I don't know, to me beautiful people are those who excel at being unique.

Those who find satisfaction in walking to the beat of a different drum… their own drum.

Those who understand that real beauty isn't bought off of a self, but blossoms from within the soul.

I wear clothes because I like them and I think I look good in them.

I like Hawaiian shirts, so I wear them.

I don't bother myself with worrying if Hawaiian shirts are in, out or project any particular image in the eyes of the beholders.

I like them, so I'm going to wear them.

I'm going to drive the car that I want, eat whatever my trusty taste buds calls for, and hang out in places where I can speak my mind…in my own words…and act the way I'm most comfortable.

Now that certainly doesn't qualify me for being one of the beautiful people of the world, but I can live with that.

I for one look forward to the "ME" '80s fading away from our world.

I sure hope that we can redefine beautiful people in something a little bit more realistic in the future.

The beautiful people of the '80s have shown us that cloning is just a bad idea.

If God wanted us to be the same, He would have created us the same as Lions and Tigers and Bears, oh, my.

I say let's put on our gray, baggy sweats and go crash an aerobics class.

Just A Thought

Animated Afterlife

I get a kick out of listening to people talk about Heaven.

We all spend a lot of time dreaming about what we hope Heaven will be like.

Of course for the un-saintly types like myself, I'll be content if they just let me through those pearly gates.

A lot of people talk of mansions in the sky, streets paved of gold and a heavenly chorus of angels.

People don't seem to realize that Heaven is for eternity – which is a little bit more than 80 years.

Mansion in the sky – for eternity? Sounds to me like house arrest.

I have my own ideas about how I want to spend my eternity.

When I finally hang up my typewriter and head for those pearly gates, I'm going to put in a formal request to St Pete that I spend my eternity as a cartoon character.

I could really get off in a Yosemite Sam, Daffy Duck, Roadrunner type of existence.

Cartoon characters are always pursuing someone or

something without any consequences for the dangers they encounter.

They fall off of high cliffs, get flattened by trains, or have huge boulders dropped on their heads... only to pop right back up and continue pursuing whatever it is they are pursuing, with even more determination.

Now that's the kind of eternity I could get excited about.

Think about it.

A cartoon character lives their eternity with very few changes in their world.

Bugs Bunny is over 50 years old.

Charlie Brown must be nearing his big four-oh!

Yet these guys haven't aged a bit.

They are still the same old lovable characters that we have loved through the years.

A cartoon character doesn't worry about money, they can eat whatever they want without blowing up like a balloon- unless that's part of the storyline, and they can get smashed by boulders and never feel a thing.

Their family and friends pretty much stay the same.

There are no parents yelling and throwing dishes.

No nasty divorces to deal with.

No brothers going off to wars.

No pressures of figuring out what you want to be when you grow up, because a cartoon character never grows up.

Hey I've already proven that I can do that.

There's no crime, drugs, pollution, poverty, bigotry or unwanted children in cartoons.

It's a pretty nice world these cartoon characters live in.

A world of unlimited consistency.

A world full of drive and innocent ambition that never changes.

Yea, you can give that mansion in the sky to someone else, thank you.

Gold streets don't impress me.

And I'm almost certain that no one wants me to join in on the heavenly chorus.

If the good Lord gives us a choice, I'd like to spend my eternity being a cartoon character.

To spend an eternity having fun in a fantasy world of playful animation.

An eternity of entertaining children, making them laugh and learning the lessons they will need in their world of reality.

That's the ticket for me.

I simply can't imagine a Heaven that could be better than that.

Just A Thought

Clearly the End

I was taking my usual walk around the city on a beautiful Saturday morning thinking about it.

As I looked at the other people, I could tell they were thinking about it too.

Nobody said anything because, well, it's just not a topic people like to talk about.

We talked about stuff like this in the '60s, but that's pretty much why everyone turned to drugs – it's not a topic you want to take sober.

As I walked around, I could tell that everyone else saw the same documentary that I saw last night.

Stands to reason – you'd think by now with over 100 channels to choose from you could find something besides MASH, Andy Griffith and Sports Center reruns.

But last night, the choice was this documentary or the NBA playoffs – and we all know that the NBA playoffs are the athletic equivalent to a soap opera … you can miss a couple of weeks and go back to find you haven't missed more than five minutes of storyline.

So I settled in on the documentary.

It explained – in quite impressive detail – how the Mayan Indians created their calendar.

Now I admit to being a bit skeptical watching these things. I mean this guy with a bunch of letters next to his name that means he's smart, points to this line of figures that I quickly jump up and scream – as if I'm rehearsing for a game show – "That's Saturday night at the Bull fights!"(a pretty decent guess, being the Mayans were in Mexico, I thought), as the smart dude explains that these figures clearly predict World War II.

Well ….. I see….. Not really …. But I don't want to look stupid here in my column. He did say 'clearly shows' that this predicted WWII and I am not going to admit that I just see 5 stick people and a bull.

As I slump back down into my chair totally humiliated at how smart this guy is, I'm also becoming upset that we are at the end of April and with all the channels on this bloody cable system, you're telling me there's not one baseball game on TV tonight?

And the real kicker comes at the end when they explain – after spending an hour explaining every event in history with great detail from a bunch of pictures of bulls and stick men, I might add – that the Mayan calendar ends on the year 2012.

Are you kidding me!?

That means the world will come to an end a few years from now?!?

I mean if they got WWII right you gotta think these Mayans knew what the heck was going on.

Of course I blow it off.

I'm guessing that the calendar is so artistically detailed and organized that the old guy who did it probably got to 2012 and dropped dead from old age.

I'm guessing that the other Mayans looked at this calendar and then at each other and shrugged their shoulders, not having any clue what this old man was doing all these years in his cave and they walked away.

But then I'm reminded of another documentary that I saw recently about a doctor in Kentucky who could go into a trans and predict the future.

This guy was so good he could name the Popes in order from the beginning of time – to the END of time!

That's right, this guy .... In 1940 something .... Could name all the Popes and has been dead-on so far even after his death. His prediction states that Benedict would be the final Pope.

WOW!

If you put the Mayan calendar and this doctor Pope guy together, it starts to get a little spooky.

Then you think, well the Red Sox did win the World Series for crying out loud.

Now I understand the look on everybody's face as I walk around downtown this morning.

As you look around the world landscape, there are so many clear signs that the Mayans may just be right, here.

And the more you think about it, the clearer the picture becomes.

I'm even starting to think that Al Gore must have some genealogical ties to the Mayans.

And if – as many have predicted – the Cubs DO win the World Series this year, I'm totally jumping on the 2012 bandwagon!

Of course the bigger question is …. Isn't nights like last night the reason you spent hundreds of dollars to fill up that shelf with DVDs?

There better be a baseball game on tonight, that's all I'm sayin'

Just A Thought

EDDIE, *Be With Me Tonight*

I could feel it as I got out of bed this morning.

The air was crawling with a thick syrup of anticipation.

As I looked out my window, I was struck at how even mother nature appeared to understand the magnitude of this day. Everything was silently still, as if life itself was holding its breath in nervous apprehension.

For weeks this day has had a big star clinging to my calendar.

As I looked out my window, I wondered how many other people had awakened on this day with the same feelings of excited pause.

How many other calendars had been following that shining star to this day?

I could sense that the world knew this was the day.

The most important day of the year.

The promise of Christmas to a child is minor league compared to this day.

Your wedding day, graduation, the birth of your child, your big career break, even the Thanksgiving when Aunt

Millie had too much of the sauce and spilled the beans on a family secret that had been suspected for years, but never revealed until then.

These milestones, though significant in their own way, pale compared to this one day.

And the agony is that this excited anticipation will have to hold out until this evening.

There will be no relief until the sun has bid us a fond farewell.

At least Christmas has the decency to quench our excited spirits while the morning sun is still fresh.

At work, everyone seems to be a bit on edge. Though no one really wants to talk about it, volumes are being said in the reserved hush of the day.

Everyone will agree that this particular day seems to slow to a gut-wrenching crawl.

Then the moment of truth arrives.

With the sun safely tucked away for another evening, I settle into my favorite chair and wait for the most important event of the year.

Tonight, Ed McMahon is going to announce the next ten million-dollar winner from that group that sells us all those magazines.

For weeks, I have quietly listened to others talk of how they have reached the final level.

How they have become one of the 'select few'.

How they have more magazines laying around the house than they will ever have time to read.

But for some reason, in my heart of hearts, I can't help but feel as if this just might be my night.

I have followed every instruction.

I have met every deadline.

I have ordered every magazine that remotely has anything to do with my meager lifestyle.

I quietly sit ready to reap my rewards.

It is time for Ed McMahon to pay up for such loyalty.

How quickly reality strikes when your numbers don't even come close to the ones being called out.

I immediately insist that the whole thing is a scam.

I also lie in bed all night wondering if it might have turned out differently had I ordered just one more magazine.

The first thing you do when you go to work the next day is take a head count. The only thing worse than losing ten million dollars would be in knowing the person who won.

With everyone accounted for, we all quickly turn our attentions to the more pressing matters... like work.

Most of us laugh over our cups of coffee that we never enter those silly contests, anyway.

We don't know anyone who really does.

As life begins to settle into the same old, same old, I become resolved to the fact that I will probably always have to work for my money.

No free rides in this life, buster.

I am determined never to enter another contest again.

Ah but then another envelope comes in the mail to

announce that I am one of the 'select few' finalists for the ten million-dollar prize if I get my order in by March 6th.

Hmmmmm …. Maybe…..

Just A Thought

A Single Parent Thought

When I sat and watched all the hoopla surrounding Cal Ripken's astonishing record of playing in 2131 consecutive baseball games, a thought occurred to me.

Cal Ripken would be the ideal spokesperson for the National Society of Single Parents.

Oh I know that Cal is a happily married man, and I realize that there probably is no such thing as the National Society of Single Parents, being that most single parents simply don't have the time to organize.

But that's the point.

Cal is an athlete who personifies the work ethics that single parents don't have an option with.

During this truly remarkable streak, we were told that Cal played the game with the flu, cold, headaches, sore knees, bad hair days, hangnails and mosquito bites.

He played in the dog days of summer and the cool chills of early spring and fall.

He played the games that were meaningless, and he played in the World Series.

No one ever asked Cal if he wanted a day off.

Cal showed up at the ball park every day to play the game, not watch it.

Of all the crazy walks of life in this world, I would guess that the single parent probably appreciates Cals record more than anyone else.

No person must deal with more issues every day than the single parent.

No person must make more decisions every day than the single parent.

And nobody goes to bed more drained every night than the single parent.

Every morning, the single parent must get up, feed the children and get them off to school before they hustle off to their own jobs.

That sounds easy enough, but try doing it when your temperature is over 100 and you are feeling miserable. Most parents have a spouse that can carry the load on days like that, but not the single parent.

The life of a single parent does not come with a lot of options.

During the course of the day, the single parent has an exhausting list of things that they must do that other parents can approach with at least some measure of security in knowing they are negotiable.

The single parent must feed the kids, get them off to school, be the breadwinner,(too often, just that), juggle the bills, and follow through with the evening chores after a long day at work…feed them, bathe them, brush your teeth.

Did you finish your homework?

You want a bedtime story?

And this doesn't even account for the emotional issues that the single parent must deal with. They know better than anyone else that the real victim in a broken marriage or death of a spouse is the children.

I've never met a single parent that wasn't dedicated to providing a stable, normal life for their children.

Unfortunately, the single parent doesn't have much opportunity to deal with the personal issues of what brought them to becoming a single parent.

Again, they do not have many options.

They simply must move forward.

The kids always come first.

Cal Ripken is an American hero.

As a baseball fan, I have no problem with that. His record is clearly the best thing to happen in baseball in a long time.

But if you really want to talk heroes, let's talk about the single parent.

The single parent will make more sacrifices in a week than Cal will in his career.

The single parent is clearly the MVP (most valuable parent) every day.

And nobody plays the game of life with more character and pride than the single parent.

Playing injured is not an option for the single parent.

I'm sure many single parents would yawn at Cal's record.

After all, they will note, he has five months off every year to rest and recover from those mosquito bites.

Cal Ripken is a shoe-in for the Baseball Hall of Fame whenever he decides to hang up his cleats and go fishing.

In the Family Hall of Fame, I think the single parents should be afforded the same recognition.

They certainly have my vote.

Just A Thought

A Driving Thought

Everywhere you go, you are bound to get into a conversation involving who the worst drivers in the world are.

Some say those lunatics out in California are the worst.

Others quickly point to the south and say that's where you'll find the idiots on wheels.

And everyone agrees that the New York city taxi drivers are masters at making driving a death wish experience.

I do believe I have heard every geological location mentioned when the topic of lousy drivers comes up.

There is not one zip code that doesn't receive its fair share of argument for dismal drivers in this fine United Interstates of America.

But let me go on record here and now and put the issue to rest. There is no doubt in my mind who the worst drivers are in America today.

It's really quite simple, really.

Drum roll please:

EVERYONE WHO DOESN'T DRIVE LIKE ME IS THE WORST DRIVER!

It really does boil down to just that doesn't it?

It pretty much depends on where you grew up and learned to drive, if you ask me.

When I moved to Nashville, I found the drivers here to be horrible.

The number one cause of death in Nashville is the four-way stop. People will sit there for days waiting on the other guy to make a move. I guess the rule is that the person to your right has the right of way. In Nashville, that means this young lady is waiting for the guy to her right, who is waiting for the guy to his right, who is waiting for the little old lady to his right, who is waiting for the young lady, who is...

Well, you get the picture.

If I wanted to be a millionaire in a short amount of time, I would put up concession stands at every four-way stop in Nashville.

I also found a lot of people who actually come to a stop at the top of a freeway on-ramp waiting for an opening. There were many occasions where I almost literally would become a back seat driver for these idiots.

Nashville drivers were way too timid for my blood.

But I grew up in southern California. A four-way stop is really a four-way yield.

And you better be going at least 55 by the time you reach the top of the on-ramp if you want to drive the interstates of southern Cal, (This of course, does not include L.A., where drivers seldom reach 55 on the interstates but, I am told, usually reach for guns instead).

If you are a timid driver in southern California, you had better carry a lot of bus tokens with you and use them!

We are all victims of driving with the attitude developed from the conditions we learned to drive in.

No matter how long I live in the south, I will always drive like a Californian.

I will never be accused of being a timid driver.

When I come to a four-way stop in Nashville, I will ALWAYS be the guy on the right.

Our cars have become a very personal part of our lives, haven't they?

We are not only very possessive of our cars, but also in how we drive them.

You can call me a fool about most everything but don't even try to tell me that I don't know how to drive my car!

Those who know me will say that I'm a real laid-back, easy-going guy.

But behind the wheel, I admit to becoming a raving maniac.

I scream at the guy in front of me for going too slow, and the idiot behind me who's riding my tail.

I don't like truckers and they don't like me.

Old people should not be driving and young people are even worse.

Rich people are snobs who think they own the road, and

poor people are an eyesore that need to stay out of my way!

And don't even get me started on those fools who mosey along with a *#!*#*!*#! phone connected to their head.

Let's face it. I don't like anyone who doesn't drive like me.

But I'm honest enough to admit that if everyone DID drive like me, the interstates would become a graveyard for fools.

I guess if you really thought about it, you'd have to say that I would be the worse driver in the world.

But then again, so are you.

Was this an issue when we had horses?

Just A Thought

Compute This

My dad loved to write letters.

He would go through a ritual of correlating typing paper with carbon papers. [for those younger than I, carbon paper is thin paper that I think was just marinated in ink such that when you typed on one sheet through the carbon paper to the other sheet, you had two copies of the same thing, as well as ink-laden fingers!]

Unfortunately, dad had six kids.

He would carefully jam six copies into his machine – that's paper, carbon, paper, carbon, paper, carbon, paper, carbon, paper, carbon, paper – and gleefully spin his tales to his beloved children.

It was actually a pretty good exercise in building family ties, because the six of us would call each other searching for the ones who got the first two copies so the rest of us could find out what the hell dad was talking about.

And if you were number six, you would call dad and tell him you loved him and ask if there was anything you could do for him because you certainly didn't want to be number six on dad's mailing list, that's for sure.

Even as the world progressed to a point where it was possible to type one letter and make five copies at the local post office, dad resisted the change.

His system worked fine, he felt, and he didn't see the need to complicate things by figuring out these new copy machines.

Dad was never a new gadgets kind of guy.

It seems like such an ancient world removed from today's technology of cut and paste, point and click environments.

But I'm not certain that our world is any easier than my dads.

In fact, as I get older, I'm thinking my dad was one smart cookie.

I have sold my soul to the wonderful world of cyber-technology.

It all seemed like a swell thing at the time.

Heck, I could have all my stories right on line for the whole world to enjoy. I could put songs on there, hook up with profitable companies and maybe make a buck or two – a huge concept for starving writers – and throw on a picture or two just for good measure.

I was a new world kinda guy, I'm tellin' ya, and I put many hours getting my web site just write so I could share it with my family, friends and all those publishers and editors who have made me the most unrecognized writer in American history!

I was set, and it was a great world I lived in. I scoffed at my dear departed dad as I pointed and clicked my way into www.anonymity.

But here's the problem.

When you have a web site, you have to get into bed with a lot of Techie people who are the kind of people who were beat up for lunch money in third grade. You know who I'm talking about. While we grew up becoming surfer dudes, party animals and generally really cool people, these techie people were reading books and becoming the forefathers of this new world of cyber technology.

They were the ones who set up the rules and you can bet the farm that they – on PURPOSE, I submit – set these rules up with only one goal and one goal only –

PAY BACK FOR ALL THE RUDE COMMENTS ABOUT POCKET PROTECTORS IN THEIR SHIRT POCKETS!

That's right ladies and gentlemen, the techie people found a way to get back at us by creating a world that truly has us reeling in a constant sea of insane procedures that have nothing to do with common sense.

In my web world, I have a server.

I have no idea what a server is.

In beach volleyball, it's the guy with the ball.

In wwweb world, it's the guy who has you by the balls.

Now I'm going to change servers – I don't know why except I'm told server #2 is cheaper and since I don't know what a server does anyway, I'm willing to pay less for it.

I cancel server #1. I call server #2 to tell them to give old Andy's site a good serve – only to find out there are about ten steps that nobody told me about that are apparently pretty darn important if you want your web site to go from one server to another.

Techie people do that on purpose.

Two months later, my web site is back and all the cyber planets are aligned correctly.

I still have no idea what I did wrong, or how I got it back.

But I go on record in saying that NEVER in my entire life have I beat up a kid for lunch money!

Techie people always use phrases like …'Didn't you ….' or 'Everyone knows you're suppose to …'

These people were watching me surf and party at the beach while they created all these secret codes that I had no idea would affect my web site so greatly.

I'm so upset because I have no idea what I'm upset about.

I only know that it was my fault, whatever it was.

I feel the need to go buy some carbon paper.

Just a Thought

The Book on George Bailey

Have you ever read any of those self-help books about being a successful person in this world?

Being a starving writer for such a long time, I would fish just about anywhere to catch a few ideas about becoming a success, so I read many of these books.

There's a lot of information in these books that I really agree with 100%.

They say if you want to be a successful person, you must believe in yourself and have a healthy, positive attitude.

I've got no problem with that.

I've always said that attitude was everything.

I'm a real Tug McGraw kinda guy. Ya gotta believe, Ya gotta believe!

If I was a baseball coach, I'd much rather work with a bunch of guys with marginal talent and unlimited desire and love for the game, than to work with a bunch of guys who had unlimited talent but marginal desire and love for the game.

I like people who see the glass as half full, not half empty.

I don't like the words can't or never.

I get real excited when someone tells me that I can't do something.

I think that people who lose but go down fighting are more successful in life than those who win without putting much heart into it.

Believe in your dreams, and do whatever you can to make them happen.

They will also tell you that the successful person will set goals and follow through with them.

I think that's a good idea, too.

I have a lot of ideas for writing that I'd like to see turned into reality. I know that none of my great ideas will materialize unless I set specific goals for them, have a game plan ready with time limits and stick with my plan until my goals are achieved.

Goals are important if you want to get things done in this world.

A person who has faith in himself, has a positive attitude, sets realistic goals for himself and follows through with them, is certainly going to be a successful person.

However, I do have a problem with one aspect of these books that seems to be consistent with this idea of being a success.

They always seem to fill the book with case histories of people who had nothing and after following this sure-fire program, became rich with a six-figure income, fur coats, large mansions and fancy cars.

Why is it that we always measure success through our bank accounts?

Of all the things we have to deal with in our travels through this wonderful world of ours, I would argue that the most fickle thing we deal with is money.

Relationships, family, religion, marriage, careers.

These are the issues in our lives that are not only more important, but are the most consistent that we have and can do more towards being considered a success than money.

Go ahead. Go to the library and check out any and all biographies about people who are financially successful. Unless their name is Kennedy or Rockefeller, you can bet that there will be a few chapters about bankruptcy, financial ruins, years of desperation, and financial headaches.

We spend way too much time associating wealth with success.

Heck, I know a lot of people who have more money than they'll ever need but they also have lousy marriages, they treat their kids awful and they never have anything positive to say about life.

They are not successful people, they are just rich people.

On the other hand, we all fell in love with George Bailey from 'IT'S A WONDERFUL LIFE'.

He never had much money, but he had a great loving family, a good positive heart, goals that he worked hard at and as we all remember at the end, he was the one they proclaimed as the richest man in Bedford Falls.

I think these books about how to be a success ought to leave money out of it.

People should believe in themselves, have a positive attitude, set goals for themselves and do what they can to reach those goals.

And if the money should come, that's fine.

But that's not the measuring stick for which we should measure ones success.

After all, we need a lot more George Baileys than we do Kennedys or Rockefellers.

Just A Thought

Losing The Last Frontier

Recently, I have become rather saddened by some of the developments that I have been reading about.

We Americans have built a long, proud history rich in adventurous pursuits of new frontiers.

We have never been a country to sit pat on anything.

We've always looked for new roads to travel.

New worlds to explore.

New frontiers to conquer.

America has always lead the way down uncharted roads.

From our forefathers heading west to explore the virgin lands of our infant country, to today's high-tech scientists exploring new methods of overcoming disease, America has always had a built in resolve to meet every challenge with a spirit of determination not to give up until victory was ours.

When the world got tired of riding a horse, America invented the car.

When the world wanted to fly like the birds, America invented the airplane.

And when teenage girls wanted to talk, America invented the telephone.

Today we face a number of environmental concerns, and you can bet the farm that it will be America who will lead the way in finding the best solutions to these problems.

But I have become concerned about our space program.

Has America's pioneering spirit of leading the world into new frontiers lost its edge?

Are we becoming so smug in our world of creature comforts to be willing to take a back seat in the pursuit of new, uncharted worlds before us?

There are many people who would say that we need to leave space alone and concentrate our efforts on some of the more immediate problems facing us today.

Although budget concerns certainly support this line of thought, I can't help but wonder if it wouldn't be a terrible mistake for us to forsake the one thing that has set our country apart from the others for all these years.

I remember when JFK told us that we would have a man on the moon by the end of the decade.

We were all quick to call it a crazy notion.

And even quicker to say, "Let's do it!"

And by God, we did it!

During the insanity of the sixties, it was the space program that served as the one positive glue that kept us all together.

We would all take time off from our riots, protests, demonstrations, LSD trips and love-ins long enough to watch another lift off at Cape Canaveral.

Everything across America would come to a halt whenever the cameras focused in on our men in space.

From the Gemini flights, the walks in space, the Apolo flights, one small step for man, the giant leaps for mankind, the Rover dune buggies buzzing around a moon crater, Alan Sheppard's golf swing, the American flag standing tall and proud amidst a barren moon's playground, and of course, those majestic splash downs in the blue Pacific.

America's space program captured the imagination and the spirit of adventure in the hearts of everyone like no other exploration ever before.

Actually, we've gotten so good at it, that the reports of our space Shuttle flights have become token side notes on our evening news.

Certainly there are many problems in our daily lives that need our attention.

Certainly our budgetary pie can only be cut into so many slices.

And yes, I too get irritated at watching millions of dollars being shot up in yet, another secret military satellite.

But we are America.

It's always been our nature to explore.

We have always improved our world by exploring the unknown worlds before us.

So many of our creature comforts of today have evolved from yesterday's commitment to conquer space.

Tang and microwaves, people!

They say that space is our final frontier.

It won't be easy… and it won't come cheap.

But I can't help but think that it will be America who will lead the way.

I know we can do it.

It's our nature to explore.

Just A Thought

Finally, It's Over

Thank God, he finally did it!

And although I can look forward to seeing it played back five thousand times over the next two days, I can at least see the light at the end of this tunnel.

Barry Bonds hit 756 last night to become the all-time home run king in baseball!

Hurray for him.

Now can we please stop watching the last place Giants and their steroid poster boy and get back into the great races that are shaping up throughout the rest of baseball?

PLEASE!

Mets, Braves, Phillies ... BrewCrew, Cubs... Pads, D'Backs ... Red Sox, Yanks ... Tigers, Indians ... Angels, Mariners .... moving into mid-August, there are some wonderful races shaping up and yet we have spent the last couple of weeks following the pathetically pitiful Giants play while their steroid star – whom NOBODY outside San Francisco likes – tries to snatch a record that NOBODY thinks he deserves.

That's two weeks of my baseball life I want back, please.

While the media goes about their usual overkill of this story, I am excited to put it behind me – way, way, way behind me as quick as I can and start putting my focus on actual SPORT stories and pennant races.

I'm a sports fan.

I love to see athletes rise up and excel to great achievements.

And if it turns out they cheated to reach that achievement, then shame on them.

They are scum bags who don't understand what sport is all about – and most sport fans will cast them out of their hearts forever.

Track 'n Field, Swimming, NASCAR, Cycling, Hockey or the big three – it doesn't matter to the sports fan.

If you achieve great levels by creating unfair advantages over the others, then you have no achievement in sport, you only have achievement in greed.

Sport fans tolerate greed on a contract, they will never tolerate greed on the field.

I'm not about to jump on any bandwagon about Barry Bonds.

Say whatever you want about him because I am a sports fan who just wants to talk baseball.

I'm not a doctor.

I have no idea how steroids work.

And I have no idea how exactly this stuff helps you play the game.

I only know that at 55 years old, the only thing that has grown since my 40th birthday is my gut, and no one has ever accused me of taking steroids for that.

So Barry now has his beloved record that has kept him out of retirement.

God bless him.

I hope he quietly retires and enjoys all he has achieved without thinking of how he achieved it.

I'm also smart enough to know this is not going to go away.

It may well be that Barry Bonds becomes just one name on a list of many of our heroes who have taken advantage of a league that looked the other way.

We will debate forever the steroid era and whether the league or the players are to blame.

Sports fans already know that answer – they both are.

At the cost of the GAME and the sports fans heart!

But the good news is that the sports fan will always understand the passion.

We don't care about the money and contracts.

We don't care about the records.

We don't care about the players on their day off.

We care about the game.

We care about the uniform that connects to our hearts.

We care about the rivalries and understand it will never be player against player, but my team against theirs.

We know the euphoria when our team exceeds expectations, and we know the devastating emptiness when our beloved team is surprisingly sent home early in the playoffs by that dreaded Cinderella team.

So celebrate Barry's home run, or curse it.

Barry Bonds means nothing to me because I am a sports fan.

I'm one fan who is eager to set my attention to the races that are shaping up.

After all, my favorite team is poised and positioned to break my heart again this year and I want to embrace every moment of it.

Say it isn't so, Joe.

Just A Thought

A Headline To Think About

It was a headline that really caught my eye.

I read it over a couple of times.

I read it out loud to make sure I heard it right.

I couldn't believe my eyes and ears.

The headline was so mind boggling that I couldn't even read the story.

I've been on this planet over fifty years and I never dreamed I'd read a headline like that.

UN REPORT BLAMES GLOBAL WARMING ON
MAN

It wasn't exactly the top story mind you, but there it was plain as day.

The United Nations studied the problem and has determined that global warming is mans fault.

Now that may not be a significant development to you, but let me tell you folks, this is a HUGE development any way you want to look at it.

What we are saying is that global warming is our own fault.

So why is that so significant?

Because since the beginning of time, we have become experts at finding ways to blame God for everything that goes screwy.

We blame God for the disappearance of the dinosaurs.

We blame God for just about every war this planet has created.

We blame God for children dying, plane crashes, job rejections, relationship failures, weight problems, our teams losing, bad economies, tests we fail, cars that won't start, dreams that don't come true and every worthless lottery ticket we hold.

No matter what you do or how you do it, you can pretty much bet that God will always get the blame when things don't work out.

That's why we have religion, right?

So we can have someone to blame for our shortcomings.

So now you're telling me that a bunch of scientists got together and went over all these charts, studies, statistics and slide shows and couldn't find ANY reason to blame God for global warming?

I am dumbfounded.

I am appalled.

I simply can't believe that there wasn't some way we could have tagged this one on God as well!

Come on, I'm not a scientist but really, couldn't we have concluded that global warming is God's fault because he has incorrectly measured the Suns ultra violet rays which inadvertently burned a hole in our ozone which created the problem?

It can't be our fault, for crying out loud… it's NEVER our fault!

This is a sure sign that the UN has totally lost it's value to the world.

It's time to close the place down and send all these people back to their countries.

If they can't do a simple thing like find a way to blame God for global warming, then what good are they?

Scientists have never liked God all that much anyway, so you'd think they'd be able to slap the global warming issue on him, wouldn't you?

What's next?

Are they going to come out and blame the polluted oceans on us, too?

And I suppose the next animal to be extinct will be our fault?

I mean if we're not careful, we may find ourselves getting the blame for a lot of crappy stuff going on in our world.

That's why I'm calling on all my faithful readers to stand up and be counted.

Write your congressmen, senators and presidents.

Write your mother, priests and ministers.

Somebody call a televangelist before it gets out of control.

If we don't let our voices be heard now my friends, we may well have to take responsibility for many of the world's problems and that's just not fair!

It's Gods fault.

It's ALWAYS been Gods fault.

It simply can't be our fault!

For these brilliant people to come out and say that global warming is mans fault is a sure sign that the world truly is coming to an end.

At least I take some comfort in knowing that we have already established that when the world does come to an end, it will be Gods fault!

They better not pin that one on us, too!

Just A Thought

The Scouting Report

For the record, I have always been in favor of this equal rights for women movement.

Actually, I think I've been rather generous with my attitude towards women.

I have often said that women were clearly the superior beings in Gods great blueprints.

God created Adam, then he created Eve...not necessarily to provide company for Adam, as some suggest, but because he wanted to improve on the model.

Yes there has been a great deal of lousy attitudes towards women, especially in the business community.

Most of us with IQs over 10 realize that there is still far too many men sitting around in their three-piece suits, in their fancy offices, receiving inflated salaries while paying five bucks an hour to some woman to do all of his work...after she brings him some coffee.

Sure women should raise hell about this kind of attitude!

They shouldn't fight for the same pay, they should get paid more if they're doing all of the work.

I have often said that this country would not be in the shape it is today if women had more control. I'm not just for a woman President... I think we NEED a woman President.

As a Catholic boy, I am strong in my opinion that the church does NOT need more priests, they need to drop the boys club mentality and let the Nuns says Mass and do whatever else the priests do.

And with three daughters, you better believe that my girls heard me preach that if they ever date a boy who thinks girls are inferior, tell them to read the Bible creation story and tell you what the last thing God created was ?

WOMAN

Even God knew he couldn't top that.

But like so many other movements that start out in the right direction and then carries things too far, the woman's movement doesn't know where to draw the line and stay within the realms of reality.

Equal pay?... you bet! Hey, they should get paid more if they do more.

Equal opportunities? Absolutely!! Women should be encouraged to pursue leadership opportunities without hesitation.

And yes, female reporters should get the same treatment as their male counterparts when covering any sporting event, (frankly, I think they should ALL stay out of the locker rooms and let the athletes shower and shave without all those microphones stuck in their faces.)

But the Boy Scouts Of America?

Come on...you've got to be kidding me!

I like what the Indians use to say. They complained a lot about white men who would hunt animals just because they were there... instead of hunting only for what you needed for food and warmth.

Sometimes the woman's movement takes on the appearance of the white hunter.

I'm a flexible guy.

I always keep an open mind on many of the world's mysteries, but I can't for the life of me understand why the women of the world would want to take on the Boy Scouts Of America?

Now for the record, I was never in the Boy Scouts...well actually, I was a Boy Scout for about a month before I got booted out. Seems I didn't want to do much except go on camping trips, but that's another story.

The point here is that I certainly do not hold any special allegiance to the Boy Scouts.

My position is strictly principal.

What is the point in watching some poor young lady being dragged into court by her parents because they want her to become a Boy Scout?

Why can't they get her involved with the Girl Scouts?

Seems to me that they would gladly accept her there.

If, as some have said, the Girl Scouts don't provide the same opportunities as the Boy Scouts, maybe these parents should be taking the Girls Scouts to court instead and demanding that they provide equal opportunities for the girls that the Boy Scouts enjoy.

I could understand that and fully support it.

I would be the first to say that there is nothing that the Boy Scouts do that the Girl Scouts should not be able to do.

But I also believe that given all this equality stuff, there is also a need to provide some sense of separate identity.

The Girl Scouts should be for girls only.

They should be able to do all the things they want to do without any boys hanging around.

And the same can be said for the Boy Scouts.

If the Girl Scouts are missing something, then let's push to fix it up.

Fight for equal pay, yes.

Fight for equal opportunities, absolutely!

And never back off your pressure to stop men's awful attitudes towards women, especially in the work force.

But let's not make a stink over the Boy Scout and the Girl Scouts.

Next thing you know, some clown is going to take on the Catholic Church so that he can become a nun.

Just A Thought

Trimming Turkeys

Thanksgiving has long been one of my favorite holidays. Simply put, I like to eat.

Setting aside a day for everyone to get together, eat a lot of food and give a thankful nod to this rat race we generously call life, really appeals to this eat, drink and be merry kinda guy.

When I was growing up, Thanksgiving was the one day of the year that we all put aside our busy social calendars and sat down together to enjoy a great feast of turkey with all the trimmings. With six active kids, the Smith family usually ate dinners in shifts, with people always coming and going to this, that and the other activities.

Mom would make a big casserole and if you were lucky enough to be available for the first shift, you ate pretty well.

Anytime after that and you were on your own.

Now keep in mind that this was before microwaves, so if you were late for dinner, it took some time and effort to bring your dinner up to palatable pleasure.

But come Thanksgiving, the entire Smith family would

be present and accounted for with our appetites deliciously synchronized to the same time zone.

There was Mom and Dad, brothers and sisters. Grandma and Grandpa Smith and Granny Dot.

Granny Dot would always bring her famous cheese cake and her sweet potatoes that mom never let us children have.

Imagine growing up in a family with a mom who would actually force you NOT to eat the sweet potatoes?!

What are the odds on that one?

Well it seems that Granny Dot liked to add a little shot or so of her favorite beverage to her sweet potatoes. The operative phrase here, of course, is 'or so'. We could all envision her meticulously following her special recipe...

A shot for me and a splash for the 'tators...

A shot for me and a splash for the 'tators.

Well them 'tators were so splashed by the time they reached our table, (as was Granny Dot, of course), that only the well-seasoned veteran of many a splash would partake in the 'tators.

It wasn't until I was an adult and went to a church Thanksgiving supper that I realized what Sweet Potatoes were SUPPOSED to taste like.

Not bad, but after all those years of the great Granny Dot sweet potato adventures, eating regular sweet potatoes just didn't feel like Thanksgiving. In total respect and admiration for my dear departed grandmother, I always seem to pass up the sweet potatoes every Thanksgiving.

Somehow, it's just not Thanksgiving unless the sweet potatoes are 90 proof.

The turkey was always the biggest that mom could find.

She was a great cook who had a real knack for making the turkey and dressing look more appetizing than those luscious Kraft Hallmark Theater commercials.

Of course there was all the trimmings to go with it, which consisted of bowls of food that you would never see any other time of the year... small creamed onions, cranberry sauce, brussel sprouts, home-made rolls and, just to keep some sign of normalcy, a bowl of good old American smashed potatoes.

Enough food to feed an army. And the Smith family was a respectable army to feed.

Before we could eat, Dad would go around the table and ask us to give thanks for something in our lives.

Mom was always practical and religious.

Dad always over-produced everything was always the greatest with dad.

My sisters were very specific and sentimental.

My brothers brief and anxious to dig in.

Grandma Smith was thankful for family.

Grandpa Smith, who was not known for his endearing tongue, hated this part of Thanksgiving and would always toss out a token thanks to that S.O.B. down at the hardware store that gave him a break on some screws he bought in June.

And Granny Dot was always thankful to be alive, which by this time in the evening was truly a valid blessing.

For me, I was always thankful that I survived another year without my brother killing me, but Thanksgiving didn't seem like the appropriate time to dig up old battles, so I usually tried to come up with something profound and sensitive to the world on a whole.

"I'm thankful that the Beach Boys new album came out with 32 days of shopping until Christmas."

Sweet Potatoes, anybody?

Just A Thought

Sleeping Through Tornados

I didn't tell anyone because it was no big deal.

I was to go to the hospital early in the morning, they would do their thing, my daughter would drive me home by noon and that would be that.

Pretty simple I thought.

Didn't sound like anything I would need a Last Will for.

My daughters were the only ones to know.

It was a nice morning as my daughter and I made our way to the early appointment to prepare me for what doctors like to call a procedure.

They were to drug me up, yet I was to remain conscience as they stuck this camera thingy down my throat to take a bunch of pictures of my insides.

Didn't sound too exciting to me, but the operative word here was 'drug', as I was assured that even though I would be alert throughout this procedure, I wouldn't feel a thing.

Sounded like the '60s to me.

Of course doctors always know what they're talking about and we got through the ordeal without a hitch.

It was a rather uncomfortable procedure, but the drugs were great.

They could have driven a Mack truck down my throat and I would have been a happy camper.

As we made our way home, I remember two things.

First, there is the lust of a beautiful woman or the lust of an anticipated feast when you're hungry, but there is no lust that compares to the lust of a pillow after a procedure like this. I could not wait to get home and snuggle into my pillow as I excuse myself from the human race for awhile.

Secondly, I noticed that the weather was quickly changing on us. It was still sunny, but the wind was whipping up what appeared to be a typical spring storm that was in the works for the afternoon.

Well this was one spring storm that would have to play without me.

I had a date with my pillow.

The next thing I remember was my daughter shaking me from my cozy unconsciousness with blurry words like tornado, basement, we're going to die if you don't get up right now, and other stuff that didn't sound all that important to me. I pretty much blew my daughter off and settled back into my slumberland.

All great things come to an end, and sure enough, I came back to life.

I aimlessly wandered around the house with no particular destination in mind.

I looked out the window and noticed that it was indeed

raining as predicted and the wind was kicking up a pretty good stir.

I found my way to my couch, where I just sat staring at the TV as if I was watching an intense game – even though it wasn't even on.

I was jarred into reality with the phone screaming at me.

My mind was telling me that I probably shouldn't answer it in this state, but my arm was already reaching for it.

"AAAAAAAAAAAAAAA hell-0"

"Andy, this is your mom just calling to see if you were alright."

My mother lives 2000 miles from me and I only told my daughters about the procedure.

That is so typical of a mother.

You can't get anything by them.

"AAAAAAAAAAAAAAA, I'm okay......You?"

"Well I heard Tom Brokaw talking about it and it sounded pretty serious."

There is a pause as I frantically reach for some logic here.

"AAAAAAAAAAAAAAA, Tom Brokaw?"

"Yes honey, it was all over the news, but I'm glad to hear you're okay."

Another long pause as I try to imagine a world so uneventful that Tom Brokaw would need to spend his newscast talking about my procedure.

"Gee mom, it was just a procedure, really."

Another pause, this time on my mother's end.

"Procedure?... It was a tornado and it looks like it went right through your area and right into downtown Nashville!"

Suddenly the skies opened up with a thunderous Alleluia Chorus as I realize just what the hell my mother is talking about.

As I explained the procedure to my mother and that I had slept through whatever it was Tom was telling her, she got a good laugh and encouraged me to go back to bed – which I did.

But I assured her that the next time I had a procedure, I would call Tom Brokaw to let him know that I'm okay.

Just in case.

Just A Thought

Take Your Best Shot

I do appreciate science.

I enjoy reading and watching stories about science.

I am always fascinated at how scientists can explain so many things about the world we live in.

I remember growing up being taught that the whole universe consisted of the sun and nine planets.

Yet just in my lifetime, we now know that our solar system is just a spec as there are millions of systems with stars and planets floating around them.

I seldom understand their explanation – how do you know that there is a planet the size of Jupiter made up of all these gasses and atmospheres when all you've actually observed is a 'wobble' in a star?

But I assume that this is why they are scientists and I am not.

It seems as if technology advances so quickly today that we are able to change the profile of life before the ink on the last profile has a chance to dry.

We have become such an advanced society that we pretty

much take these daily stories of discovery and explanations from science with an emotional yawn.

Whether you buy into it or not doesn't really matter because we know that it will likely all change again next week when they discover something new.

Part of the new science of today's world involves our history.

Specifically, there seems to be more and more theories and explanations coming out about the Bible.

Though there are many Christians who become defensive about these stories, I have no problem with them. I understand that science doesn't sleep well until they have a logical explanation for everything.

Of course, these are the same people who smugly proclaim that a mere wobble in a distant star clearly proves that there is a planet out there the size of Jupiter composed of all these gasses and atmospheres.

Interesting theories? – yes.

Clear Proof? – not so much.

But I'm not smart enough – as the rest of us non-scientists – to prove them wrong, so we common folk pretty much let them have their spotlight and their expertise on the matter.

If they want to explain every miracle Jesus performed, I say knock yourself out.

Though the miracles are important and add to our foundation, my faith does not depend on whether Jesus walked on water or ice, or whatever they 'think' they know.

If they want to explain Noah's ark, the splitting of the Red

Sea, or even come up with manuscripts that suggest Jesus and Judas had some deal set up, I'm going to have to respond again – knock yourselves out.

Though I trust these stories in the Bible to be true, it will never change my faith if they come up with anything that suggests that these stories may not be exactly as they appear.

I only have two points to say about all this.

First, we must always keep in mind that history was documented much differently than it is today.

There was no CNN, satellite imagery or internets.

There was no Office Depot down the street with stacks of paper waiting to be filled.

There were two ways of documenting historic events of those days.

For most, it was passed from generation to generation verbally. It was very important for one generation to pass on the stories of family history and the events that molded their lives to the next generation.

The other way was to write it down. Paper – or parchment as it is referred to – was not readily available at the time and it is generally understood that you simply didn't write down the events unless it was very important to future generations. The process was so arduous that it simply had to be important and accurate to warrant such effort.

With this, I have to believe that the stories in the Bible are pretty accurate and representative of the events that took place two thousand years ago.

That being said, I will go back to the scientists and say

that until you can prove the resurrection did not happen or explain it in some manner other than the documentation we have in the Bible, my faith will never be shaken.

Without the resurrection, Jesus was just a martyr.

Without the resurrection, Jesus' teachings were not all that different from any other prophet or religious leader.

Without the resurrection, Christianity is just another religion.

The resurrection is the absolute point of faith for all Christians.

The Bible is careful to document that this was not a ghost, but that Jesus had the disciples touch his wounds and ate fish with them.

Though both the Jewish and Roman leaders of the day had great incentive – and resources – to prove the resurrection did not happen, neither one was able to come up with anything that suggests that the Bible stories are wrong or inaccurate.

So go ahead scientists and prove what you will.

But until you can prove that Jesus did not resurrect from the dead, my Christian faith will never weaken.

And you'll have to give me a lot more than a wobble explanation, that's for sure.

Just A Thought

'Nuff Said

Sometimes you read a headline and it just pulls you to the story.

That's what a good headline is supposed to do.

It's supposed to give you just enough information to perk your curiosity enough to read the story.

A really good headline will not reveal anything of what the story is about until AFTER you read the story. Once you've read the story, you can go back and look at the headline again and smile, "Oh I get it …. Clever!"

The fellow who wrote that headline earned his paycheck to be sure.

Headlines are an art form.

Most headlines are cookie cutter, vanilla, poorly conceived headlines that do nothing to entice the reader to the story.

Most give you too much information that causes you to think, "I already know what that's about", and you move on.

For instance, if you're a sports writer, you should NEVER have the initials T.O. in a headline.

'Athlete again validates inferior IQ'... would work much better.

I say this because I read a headline the other day that has entertained me immensely without having any idea what the story is about.

I saw this headline on a respectable web site and have not bothered to go to the story to find out what it means.

I have no desire to find out.

The headline is enough for me.

Lesbian Teens Have Greater Pregnancy Risks

Just writing that headline leaves my fingers speechless.

I consider myself a very creative thinker, yet this headline takes me nowhere.

I have no idea how to respond to this headline.

I have no idea what this story is about, nor do I have any desire to find out.

The headline alone will entertain me for weeks, I am certain.

When I first read this headline, I thought that this would make a great story idea for my column. In my first draft I wrote the headline at the beginning and then paced around my apartment for an hour to come up with my next line. When I finally got back to my computer, I wrote ... 'nuff said .... and was done.

I had nothing that could top that headline.

Now maybe this story is serious in nature and I am wrong to make light of it.

Maybe there is some scientific study that would be of value to our understanding.

Maybe if I actually read the story it would be clear to me that this headline is perfectly logical.

But I'm guessing that if this story has anything to do with teen pregnancies, lesbians would be part of the solution not part of the problem, right?

Am I just a writer who once again validates inferior IQ?

Did my Dad leave out something in our discussion about birds and bees?

Is everyone else laughing at me because I'm laughing at this headline?

When it comes to stories of sexual content, I fully understand that my name has never been associated with being the voice of authority.

In fact, if I remember right, when my Dad did sit down to explain the birds and the bees to me he stared at me for some time as I sat there with my long hair dripping from the ocean playground, smiling in clueless innocence as he mostly discussed the benefits of choosing a life of service to the church.

The Pope could use more priests is what I recall.

Well I may not be the voice of authority when it comes to sex, but as a writer I sure know a good headline when I see one.

This headline was almost too good.

It stands alone.

You can giggle for weeks without ever knowing what the story was actually about in the first place.

I don't even want to know what the story was about.

The headline will entertain me for some time.

Lesbian Teens Have Greater Pregnancy Risks.

'nuff said

Just A Thought

Pets Are Animals, Too

I like pets!

I say this because I do not have any pets and have been accused of not being a pet lover.

Some of best memories from my youth are littered with pets.

My family had lots of pets.

Not necessarily by choice, mind you.

My parents were not the kind of people to keep the veterinarians phone number close by.

In our house, all pets were well fed, loved and allowed to travel through their nine lives playing whatever hand Mother Nature would deal them.

This policy of course meant that our house often looked like the first chapter of Matthew. We had so many 'begets' running around that the family trees represented quickly became part of the National Forestry Service.

Needless to say, our pets did not practice safe sex.

I remember one time when one of our cats and two of our

dogs turned our home into a yelping maternity ward at the same time.

If we had to pass out cigars every time our pets gave birth, the Smith family would have provided more financial security to Cuba than any country on this fair planet.

For the most part, all of our pets were mutts.

When one of our females was in heat, the entire animal kingdom of male persuasion would gladly drop by and donate a few of their prized chromosomes for the cause.

When a Smith pet came full term, we would all hover around, curious to see what this batch of gene splicing had created.

We had one dog that was part toy poodle and part dog. She produced a number of fluffy little balls that I believe my dad sold off as key chains.

Then we had a bunch of dogs that were definitely of the German Shepherd background.

My favorite was one named Bo.

This dog put dumb on the map.

He had the most beautiful blonde coloring with droopy ears and a tongue the hung down the side of his mouth.

He actually caught his tail on fire one time when he laid too close to the floor furnace. With everyone yelling at him in a state of panic, Bo calmly put out the fire by wagging his tale in delight at all the attention he was receiving.

To this day, I believe that Bo had no clue of what everyone was yelling at him for.

We had lots of cats, but we didn't name any of them.

It's a waste of time to name your cat.

They never respond to names.

When it's time to eat, all you have to do is yell, "Here kitty, kitty, kitty", and they will be at your feet as if shot from a cannon.

Otherwise forget it.

Tell them to sit up, roll over or go fetch, and they will look at you as if you had insulted their intelligence.

Cats don't need names.

They don't want names.

They want to be fed and left alone to ravage through your home in their own manner.

I had a dog that became a mascot for the music group that I performed with. He was a mutty little mutt with not one redeeming attractive feature about him. He wasn't smart enough to do tricks, but he wasn't dumb enough to be very entertaining, either.

But he was a good friend that lived with us at our beach house and went with us to all our concerts.

Today, I am without pets for two reasons.

First, we live in a condo that I don't think is an attractive place to raise pets that need lots of room to run.

And secondly, I have three teenage daughters that do a fine job of tying up my finances and attention.

I'd love to have a dog, but only if it had a nice yard to run and play in.

I wouldn't mind having a cat, but then again, I already

have three teenagers around to ignore my commands...why do I need a cat?

Now I know that I have left out our beloved birds, fish, turtles, hamsters, rabbits and other creatures that have been considered pets by others. But I have never owned any of these creatures, so I will respectfully refrain from making any comments about these animals that I know so little about.

Come to think about it, however, I realize that I do have a pet.

I have a peeve.

In fact, I have several pet peeves.

But that will have to be another column down the road, I suppose.

Just A Thought

The Ladies of Baseball

Those who know me know that I am a big time baseball fan.

When I was just a little guy, playing baseball was the only activity on my list of things to do.

If anyone needed Andy, they knew the first place to look was down at the sandlot where it was a good bet to be the only place to look.

I loved baseball.

In my youth I would say that my game was eighty percent love and twenty percent talent.

I'd play any position and any game that required a bat and glove.

Every day was wrecked with disappointment as the sunset forced us to put away our mitts for another day.

I was not a romantic, I was a ball player and for me sunset was the worst part of the day.

When my family moved to San Diego, my game faded quickly from participation to appreciation as my teen years moved me into a world of surfing and playing music and baseball became a great night at the ball park watching my Pads.

The Padres were a young franchise.

They played horrible and looked even worse in those taco bell uniforms.

But I loved going to the games.

Watching the Big Red Machine, Mays and McCovey, and oh those dreaded Dodgers.

If the Pads won, it was a great night.

If they didn't, well it was baseball and it was the Padres after all.

My favorite player of all time was Tim Flannery.

For a teen growing up in San Diego, Tim was the coolest of cool.

It was said that he played baseball because it gave him his days to go surfing.

And when Trader Jack McKeon came to San Diego, it was said that Tim went to Jack and simply told him that if he traded him, he would retire. He was a San Diegan who loved the Pads and the city… loved to surf and had a landscaping business. He would not play for any other team.

Two years later, Tim was the only veteran Padre who was still left on the team.

I share all this with you because it leads me to my point of this story.

I wanted to talk about my mom, it being Mother's Day and all.

You see, most people would read the start of my story and

think, 'Well let's see here. His Dad was a big sports fan and he had three older brothers, so he certainly had a lot of influence with sports.'

My Dad was a big sports fan to be sure.

But none of my brothers got into any sports when they were growing up.

If you were to ask me where I get my love for baseball, I would not hesitate in saying that I got it from the females on my family tree.

Specifically, my mother and her mother.

Granny Dot (Dorothy to the rest of you) was my grandmother.

She loved baseball.

When she was nearing the end of her travels on this planet, we would go to visit her. She could never get our names right or who had what children. With six of us and several great-grandchildren, you certainly could not fault the woman.

However, if you asked her ANYTHING about the Pads, she would know the answer.

She may not have known who she was talking to exactly, but she could certainly let you know that Tony Gwynn went two for three last night and is now hitting .327.

The story of her passing is that she slipped into a semi-conscience state and the doctors were just waiting for her to let go of life.

When my mother visited her on that last night, she leaned over and whispered to her that the Pads won, breaking an eight game losing streak.

Granny Dot smiled and said, 'That's nice' and let go of life.

Nobody challenges that story because we know what kind of fan Granny Dot was.

We have no doubt that she refused to leave this planet while the Pads were losing.

We're also certain that God would not have wanted to deal with her any time sooner.

My mom took over where Granny Dot left off.

I live in Nashville now and I am well aware that come spring, I need to have my Padres schedule close by because you do not want to call mom when the Padres are playing.

And when you do talk to her, she is a great mother who loves her son and her grandchildren, to be sure … but when you mention the Padres, the level of excitement in her voice is always elevated and she can talk all day about her boys at Petco Park.

She clearly is the best Padres fan in San Diego.

So when you ask me where I got my love of the game, I always think of mom and Granny Dot.

I called mom to wish her a Happy Mother's Day on Saturday after the Pads won again.

Good thing, too.

Today St Louis is pounding the Pads.

I'm thinking it wouldn't be a great phone call right now.

Just A Thought

Heroes of My Youth

Someone asked me recently whom my heroes were when I was growing up.

I thought for a moment.

Politicians, sports figures, movie stars, rock 'n roll singers.

They were all out there.

But that's the problem.

They were out there in a world known to me only by watching the news or reading the papers... two activities I did not participate much in when I was a youth.

The real heroes in my youthful years were the guys I use to meet at that vacant lot down the street every day for an afternoon of baseball.

I love baseball.

As far back as my rusty memory will go, I can remember having my mitt close by wherever I went.

I was the kind of kid that would come home, throw down my books, grab my mitt and head down to the vacant lot where my buddies and I would squander the afternoon playing three flies up, work-up or, if there were enough of us, a real game of baseball, played with the intensity of the 7th game of the World Series.

There were the Goodwin brothers...Martin and David.

Most of us would get excited when David had to stay behind and work at his father's store. He was older than the rest of us and he always insisted on pitching, which we didn't care for because he threw so hard the rest of us didn't have a chance.

Sandlot baseball was never meant for pitcher's duels.

Marty and I were close friends.

We played on every team together until I moved to San Diego in my sophomore year of high school and traded my mitt for a surfboard.

From the Little League Champion Cardinals, the Pony League Giants, to the Rim High Scotts, Martin Goodwin and Andy Smith were always ready to get their uniforms dirty.

There was Alan Fuller and Fred Weddington.

They were pretty good ballplayers, but as the years went on, they were the ones who were anxious to wrap the game up so that they could go down to the roller rink and check out the 'babes'.

Chip Murphy was always ready to play ball.

He was fun to have on your team.

All you needed was a first baseman and Chipper would take care of the rest of the infield.

No matter where you hit the ball on the ground, that little guy would be on top of it and have it in the first baseman's glove before you got past the pitcher's mound.

It wasn't until my freshman year at high school that I finally got to play on the same team with Chipper. He played short stop and I played second. Coach Beresford would always tell us that we would be the best double play combination in Rim of the World High School history by the time we graduated.

The move to San Diego ended that, but I have no doubt that the coach would have been right.

Chipper was simply the best.

George Tage was the kid that we always tried to leave out of the games.

He was the only kid I knew who would show up for a pick-up game in full catcher's gear.

We always let him play because he had all the really good equipment.

He was a little guy.

When he walked, the chest protector would drag on the ground, and his chin guards covered his thighs as well.

What George gave up in size, he more than made up with determination.

His temper would always end the friendly game.

He didn't argue a call, he would make a tackle that would do a linebacker proud and proceed to beat the hell out of anyone who dared to go against his grain.

Playing baseball with George was far too dangerous.

Sherman Moffitt was our big gun.

We called him the Sherman Tank.

He was one of the most intimidating figures when he stood up at the plate.

A big, friendly guy with a gentle smile that contradicted the intensity in which he played the game.

As long as the Tank was on your team, baseball was a great game to play.

There were others who would show up from time to time, but these were the staples of my youthful sandlot career.

They were my heroes because they made it possible for me to spend my afternoons doing what I loved the most...play baseball.

I have no idea what ever became of these heroes of my youth.

None of them ever appeared on the cover of Sports Illustrated or Time magazine... but then, none of them ever appeared on the wall of my local Post Office, either.

Wherever they may be, I know that they too, can look back on those early days on the vacant lot down the street and remember how we use to play baseball the way it was meant to be played.

Well, all of us but George.

Just A Thought

It's A Good Song

They had a discussion the other day of what the best song ever written is.

They had the usual suspects based on the usual silliness.

Of course the whole discussion was subject to personal taste and therefore pretty much a waste of time.

As a writer the measuring stick is always to ask what emotion the song was designed to ignite and has nothing to do with ANY commercial response.

But it got me thinking.

Certainly for me there is only one song in this discussion:

"Take Me Out To The Ball game" is clearly the greatest song ever created!

A very simple song with a warm melody that anyone can sing.

And at baseball games across the country, people stand in the middle of the 7th inning to sing this wonderful song. Regardless of what's happening on the field, this song perfectly reminds us of how baseball is the best way to spend a nice summers evening. Win or lose this song always anchors us and reminds us of why we love this game so much.

None of the other sports have a song that does that.

Only baseball.

But there's another song that has my vote.

It's a song that pretty much breaks every rule of songwriting.

If I pitched this song on Music Row, the publishers would laugh me out of Nashville.

Most people can't sing the song.

A lot of people want to replace the song with another one that's easier to sing.

Of course I'm talking about our national anthem, the Stars Spangled Banner.

One of the perks of living here in Nashville is that you can go to any sporting event and you'll never hear the Star Spangled Banner sung poorly.

That's what makes us Music City USA.

Every season, every sport has auditions for people who want to sing the national anthem before their games. The lines are always long with recording artist wantabes anxious to stamp their resume with this challenging opportunity.

And don't kid yourself – singing the national anthem in front of thousands of spectators at a sporting event is not a bad item to have on your resume, that's for sure.

While choppy and poorly structured, the lyrics remind us of our infant struggles and how, even in our darkest hour, our flag was still there.

The music, though melodically difficult, creates a feeling of hope, pride and loyalty.

Together, the lyrics and music of our national anthem reflects perfectly what our country is all about; it's a difficult song to sing, but when performed right, it's full of pride built on a strong foundation of hope.

When you watch the Olympics, most of the other countries have national anthems that reflect a sense of strength and loyalty.

They almost all have a military feel to them designed to build loyalty through strength.

Not ours.

We build our loyalty through hope by standing tall in our darkest hour.

By waving our flag majestically in the face of terrible odds.

By refusing to let adversity destroy our spirit.

I always sing loud and proud at the 7th inning stretch at a baseball game.

I never sing the Star Spangled Banner– I don't want to ruin a good thing.

But in many respects, that's a good thing; if you quietly let those who can handle it sing our national anthem with the strength and skills God gave them, it's the kind of song that can draw you inward to reflect on how fortunate we all are to be Americans.

I always have tears in my eyes at the beginning of sporting events.

Now that's the perfect national anthem.

And that's what makes it the best song ever.
Or the second best, if you are a baseball fan.

Just A Thought

It's All About Fads

I figured out what it is that separates the human race from the rest of the animal kingdom.

That special something that makes us so different from the wonderful world of Lions and Tigers and Bears, oh my;

Fads

The life of a Monkey in the 1990's is probably not much different from the life of a Monkey in the 1890's.

But not so the humans.

We can identify time in history by its fads. Fads consume almost every part of our lives. In fact I can't think of any area of our lives that is not controlled by fads. It's in the clothes we wear, the food we eat, the things we say. It controls the way we fix our hair, the way we play and the way we spend our money. And even if you are a fad-hater, you will probably not be able to get through the day without it controlling some of what you do.

Every generation is identified by its fads.

I was a teenager during the 60's.

I am identified with paisley shirts, bell-bottom jeans, "far-out", battle-of-the-bands, marijuana, flower-power hippies and protests.

It doesn't matter to what degree, if any, I participated in these fads, I was a kid in the 60's and these fads are what affect my lifestyle even today.

As a parent with three young ladies, I often hear one of my children say, "But everybody's wearing them" as they plead with me for a new set of stitches.

Of course I always respond right out of the parental response manual, "But you're not everybody!"

Some poor lady had to sew patches on her child's' jeans because she was too poor to buy new ones. Now as she finally is able to go buy those jeans, she desperately holds her tongue as her daughter hands her a pair of fifty dollar jeans that have patches sewn on them. Before dear old mom can say anything, her loving child looks to her and says, "But everybody's wearing them".

For a struggling writer who is not shy to point out my genius whenever I can, I try to convince my girls that they should try to be trend setters.

A trendsetter can do whatever they want.

They can buy a funny looking hat if they want to.

They wear it to school a few times and pretty soon everyone else is running around looking for that same hat for themselves.

I remember when I was in high school I belonged to a club that had a rule that members had to wear a tie every Tuesday. My dad had a bow tie that I thought would be kind a different, so I started to wear it on Tuesdays. Well at first everyone thought I had a bad reaction to some dried banana skins, but before long, guys were coming up to me and asking where they could find a bow tie. My mom made a bunch of them from old Hawaiian shirts and I sold them for a buck a piece. Soon everyone in the club wore bow ties every Tuesday.

Not only can being a trendsetter be less stressful, it can also be profitable.

But it doesn't always work out that way.

My daughter got some penny-loafer shoes (everybody was wearing them, you know). She was searching high and low for a couple of pennies to put in those slots they have. I gave her my speech about being a trendsetter and starting her own fad. I told her to put a couple of dimes in the slots and when the people asked, tell them that she's worth more. She tried it, but nobody noticed her dimes and after a few weeks, she spent the dimes and resorted back to putting pennies in her shoes.

Fads are what give us our character.

You either follow or you rebel against a fad.

The fad never loses.

By the time we realize that the fad is silly, it's too late. The fad has already made its mark in history and will only be replaced by another silly fad.

Maybe the Monkey, along with our Lions and Tigers and Bears, are right.

Without fads, their lives seem to be a lot more relaxed and carefree.

But then again, maybe I'm just a parent with three girls crashing in on their teens.

After all, I still hold on to my black and white saddle-oxford shoes and bow ties that made me a legend in my own mind back when I was a brain-dead teen.

I hope that my girls can come up with something better, though.

Just A Thought

Expand This!

I am bewildered by all the fuss going on about the tasteless halftime entertainment at the recent Super Bowl.

Even Congress is holding hearings, debating for hours the horrors of exposing our innocent children to a quick donning of a breast.

We are talking about something that happened so fast, it pretty much missed most of the chips 'n dips society.

Those who were actually paying attention raised their eyebrows, looked at others in the room and asked, 'Did I just see what I think I just saw?' Everyone shrugged their shoulders in a glazed fog and then headed for the fridge for another beer.

Don't get me wrong, I am in no way condoning what this entertainer did. I go on record here in saying that the only talent in today's Pop culture is in the ability to raise the bar of tasteless.

Shocking the audience is so much more profitable than actually entertaining us.

But that's not what I want to talk about today.

What I'm talking about is taking back our TVs.

Forget the breast ladies and gentlemen, and let's talk about taking back our TVs before it totally gets out of control.

It seems to me that the marketing monsters have determined that they have a right to take over the bottom third of our TV screens. Every time I sit down to watch a program in the privacy of my home, I find that the 27 inch screen that I chose as the right size for my viewing tastes is now an 18 inch screen with a scrolling bottom third throwing annoying information at me that I never asked for, have no interest in, and is frankly quite distracting in my ability to watch the program I chose to watch.

We have weather updates, headline news, sports updates and programming notes that the marketing monsters throw at us whether we want it or not.

And don't think for a minute that they are going to stop there.

Once we get acclimated to this new trend in annoyance, you can be assured that the glutinous marketing monster will expand to a point where we may find ourselves turning on the TV to watch a program, only to find some slick-willie informing us that we really don't want to watch said program, so instead, we will throw this wonderful marketing crap at you.

It's time to take back our TVs people!

And your old buddy Andy has the perfect solution.

I have, as most of you do, a remote for my TV that has about a billion buttons on it, of which I understand what three of them do. It seems to me that the people who make TVs love to make remotes with buttons – lots of buttons – lots and lots of buttons that we, the consumers will never figure out.

I'm saying it's time to give us a button that we all can understand and get very good use out of.

I say it's time to put an 'expand' button on our remotes.

Here's how it works:

In my community, every winter when there is a snow flake sighting, our local channels will immediately take over the bottom third of my screen to keep me informed of Mother Natures furry. There will be maps and endless lists of schools that have frantically closed their doors.

This is good information for parents who need to know if they should wake junior up, but since my juniors have left the nest, I am not all that concerned if schools are open or not- nothing against the schools, I just don't need that information.

I should be able to push my 'expand' button and let my 27 inch screen provide me the 27 inch program I want to see.

No hard feelings, I'm just not interested, thank you.

Our computers now come with all kinds of armor to stop unwanted spam, pop-ups and other annoyances brought to you by those glutinous marketing monsters, whose motto is, 'We don't care'.

Why can't we have an 'expand' button on our remote to stop unwanted intrusions on our TVs?

Yes, the halftime entertainment was certainly tasteless.

But let's go after the real monsters here.

People have the right to watch whatever they want in the privacy of their homes.

They should also have the right to say no every time their 27 inch screen becomes an 18 inch screen.

Just a thought

Freedoms Price Tag

YOU NEVER SAID YOU WERE PERFECT,
YOU ONLY SAID YOU WERE FREE.
I THANK YOU FOR TRYING SO HARD
TO KEEP IT THAT WAY FOR ME.

These lines came from a song I wrote for America's bicentennial back in 1976.

As we celebrate another year of being the melting pot of the world, I thought it'd be nice if I shared with you what I think about when I think about this country of ours.

When the oppressed cram into boats to get away from their broken homelands, it's America that their hearts always pointed to.

You can see the greatness of America when you go to the library. There are rows of biographies about people who come from humble, often times awful backgrounds, and become great achievers and valuable contributors to our world.

Most countries cannot offer you those stories.

The homeless family in Mississippi has as much say in

whom our next leaders will be as the affluent family in Beverly Hills.

A country where dreamers are still encouraged to take their best shot.

A country where a baby girl is not closed down and rendered a second class citizen, but can reach for her stars, wherever they may shine.

Where freedom is sacred... even to those who would abuse it.

Where belief in God can be freely expressed, no matter how far off the beaten path it may be.

America... A country that has been bruised so many times but continues to keep growing and moving forward.

I was a teenager during the 60's.

This was a time when America threw up.

We were protesting wars, burning our draft cards, flags and cities, shooting our President, Senators and Civil Rights leaders, smoking pot, promoting free sex and generally challenging everything that the "Leave-It-To-Beaver" generation worked so hard to preserve.

Ah, the 60's... America at it's worst... and America at it's best.

That's what I like about this country.

We go through some pretty awful times that would devastate other countries. But in America, these trying times always seem to make us all the stronger.

We didn't survive the Civil War, we came out stronger because of it.

We didn't survive the gangster days of prohibition, we came out stronger because of it.

We didn't survive the 60's, we came out stronger because of it.

And you can be certain that America will not just survive the environmental issues and any other issues that we face today or in the future, but it will lead the way in helping the world come out better because of it.

Sure, as a writer I could write volumes on the many infractions that this country stumbles through.

I could write a column about what is wrong with this country and have enough material to keep the column in ink for a long, long time.

But the truth of the matter is that all the flag burners, protesters, fanatic groups and odd-balls do not condemn this country nearly as much as they reflect what is good about this country.

Why those boats full of oppressed people still point to the shores of America for more than 200 years.

They call it freedom for ALL.

Yes America, you never did say that you were perfect... and you are not.

You only told us that you were free.

I really am thankful that you've worked so hard to keep it just that way for someone like me.

Happy Birthday.

Just A Thought

Giving Thanks

Like so many things we do in this crazy world we call life, Thanksgiving started out as a nice idea with pure intentions, but somehow became an unattractive marketing monster.

The first Thanksgiving, we are told, was a time of celebration and fellowship between the Native Americans – who were the first to call this home, and the pioneers – who were settling into the land they would call home for the first time.

It was a time of thanksgiving between two very different cultures. Two diverse people sharing one meal in celebration of shared knowledge, friendships and struggles as they carved their spirits into a new frontier.

Actually, we know that Thanksgiving was really the idea of Abe Lincoln after the civil war with the metaphor of Indians and pioneers coming together in a new world that would be perfect in his attempt to bring the country back together again.

What a nice idea – the kind of idea that should be passed along through all generations, right?

Once again, like so many other traditions, Thanksgiving seems to have lost a great deal of its original spirit through the years.

One of the things that bugs me the most – and trust me, as I get older, almost everything bugs me – is the lack of appreciation we show one another.

We have become a society that keeps its focus on what is wrong instead of appreciating that which is right.

As I look around, I am saddened by how much of this is going on.

We adults are quick to point out the sins of our youths, yet slow to acknowledge the many benefits our young people bring into our community.

We parents are quick to pile on the stiff rules and regulations with our children, yet seem to never have enough time to give them hugs and tell them how much they are appreciated.

Marriage has become an endangered species because it is easier to focus on what is wrong, run through a divorce and then crack jokes about your ex at social gatherings, than it is to focus on what's right with a marriage and work on making it better.

If you don't go to my church, you must not be right with God.

If you don't walk the same path as I, then you must be lost.

Even when we pray, we look at all that's wrong and ask God to fix it, instead of what's right and thanking Him.

Why is it so hard for us to appreciate the diversity of our existence?

We are not all blondes.

We do not all drive Fords.

We do not all love the Beach Boys, (though I can't imagine any sane person not liking them!)

One person might love an evening at the ball game yelling for the home team with a beer, hot dog and peanuts.

Another would prefer an evening at the theater.

One person might love to spend an evening wrestling with their kids.

Another would prefer to quietly snuggle up with a good novel.

One person feels closer to God in a conservative, Sunday service.

Another feels closer to God at an emotionally charged revival.

Why do we spend so much of our energies trying to justify our lives by making every other person's life wrong?

God help us if we were all like Andy Smith.

Trust me, I'm a heck of a guy, but one of me is more than enough for this world, thank you.

The Pilgrims didn't tell the natives to wear top hats, black and white formal attire and shoes with goofy looking belt buckles on them, did they?

Of course not.

It was a come as you are party.

They were celebrating their diversity as much as their common experiences.

Thanksgiving today is much different.

We all gather together, stuff our faces with a bunch of food we will never see the rest of the year, and scramble off to get a jump on those Christmas shopping specials, or watch a bunch of football games that, for the most part, means very little to us.

In most homes, there is more tension and anxiety than warmth and love being served at Thanksgiving.

I don't think that is what our forefathers were thinking about when they created this holiday.

Robert Redford once said that Earth Day was a nice idea but if we only thought about the good of our planet one day each year, we were already in big trouble.

I feel the same way about Thanksgiving.

Maybe if we all spent a little more time looking at all the good in our world, the good in our world might have a real chance to grow.

Saying thank you is the purist form of love.

Said with sincerity, it is the most powerful.

It's Thanksgiving – so say thank you, already!

Just A Thought

Gods Greeting Cards

Everybody enjoys getting a greeting card from a friend.

A simple note to say thanks, hang in there, or glad you were born, these gestures often provide the lift in spirit that can truly make our day.

You can spend a lot of money on gifts that will soon fade into lost memory, but a greeting card from family and friends always holds on to our hearts.

I find it very difficult to throw greeting cards away.

I always come across little stacks of cards that I have stashed away in a drawer that serves as a pleasant reminder of how people do think of me enough to send their thoughts.

But the absolute best greeting cards come without stamps.

And in a world that can be so hectic and busy, I'm sorry to say these greeting cards are very often not opened.

Last night I had to stop at the store on my way home from work. It was a Monday and, well, what can be said about our jobs on a Monday?

As I got out of my car, I noticed through the lifeless trees of late winter, one of the prettiest sunsets I have ever seen.

Puffy clouds scattered about were bright with pinks and silvers as the Sun made a glorious farewell to another day.

I was so captured by it, I decided to stand in the parking lot and take it in for a few moments.

You don't get a lot of sunsets like this and it's always a good idea to stop and embrace it when you do.

I noticed something that bewildered me, however.

As I was standing there enjoying the moment, there were many of my neighbors scurrying about from their car to the store and back again. I noticed that not one other person looked up to see this wonderful greeting card from God. Everyone was in too much of a hurry to take time and open their greeting card from God.

How sad.

None of us really like Mondays, yet here God was giving us a wonderful greeting that few people noticed.

It was a note of inspiration, for sure.

As if God was telling us that we made it through another Monday, so isn't life grand!

The very next morning, I slumbered into the kitchen to grab my morning cup of bring-me-back-to-life coffee.

As always, I stood at my kitchen window and stared out into the fresh new day, waiting for my eyes to moisten enough for me to focus on the scene.

And what a scene it was.

Another greeting card.

Even with the daybreak, there was the fullest of full Moons

just above the tree tops, majestically glowing against the deep blue morning sky.

We get a full Moon once a month – kind of a flashlight for God to check on us I suppose.

By the time we grab our cup of coffee in the morning, the Moon is long gone. But this must be a slow Moon this month, because it greeted me this morning in all its glory.

It was a beautiful way to start the day.

I stood there with my coffee and simply took in the beauty of it.

I wondered how many people would notice this greeting card today?

Gauging from what I saw last night at sunset, I'm thinking few people would come to work talking about the sunset or the morning Moon.

In fact, I suspect I will be the one who enthusiastically asks others if they saw the wonderful greeting cards from God and get looks from my peers as if the old man has finally lost his marbles.

No wonder so many people are depressed.

God keeps sending us greeting cards and nobody opens them.

Too bad.

It's put me in a really good mood and it's only Tuesday.

But then, that's what greeting cards are suppose to do, right?

Just a Thought.

Different Strokes

I went to a bar the other night with a friend. He knew the band that was playing and they needed someone to man the door and collect the cover charge.

Being that my daughter was having a bunch of ladies over to spend the night and celebrate her 18th, I thought this would be the perfect opportunity to get out of my daughter's way and still have a good time.

Let me tell you something, Andy Smith showing up at this bar was like Ted Kennedy showing up at a Pat Buchannon rally, a Chevy pulling into a Ford parking lot, Madonna showing up at a Baptist Women's luncheon, or wearing paisley with plaid.

Not that I'm complaining.

I've never been much of a conformist, so being the odd man out doesn't bother me.

But I must say that I was a bit hesitant when I walked into this world.

This was a beer joint.

A wine spritzer seemed out of the question.

I drank seven up.

Big cowboy hats seemed appropriate well.

My San Diego Charger baseball cap didn't work.

Several times guys walked by me and called me Bubba.

I smiled a lot in fear.

I kept cleaning my glasses thinking they were smeared, only to realize that it was merely the haze from all the smoking.

I took enough second-hand smoke to bring back memories of L.A.

And it didn't take long for me to realize that I wouldn't have much to contribute to any conversations of the evening.

I pretty much listened and observed while I drank my seven up.

What I heard and what I observed was certainly an education for this old city boy.

It's funny how your first impressions are always your worst impressions.

When I walked into this bar, I quickly convinced myself that I was going to die.

I would end up on tomorrow's front page.

"OUT OF PLACE DUDE FALLS VICTIM TO RED-
NECK BAR"

Just as quickly, I realized that I was a tad over-anxious about all this.

The truth is that these people made me feel very welcomed in their world.

Though clearly from a different life style than mine, these were nice people.

Hard workers who gathered every Saturday night to let their hair down with beer, cigarettes, loud music and, most importantly, their friends.

Everyone was having fun.

No one seemed put out by my presence.

I was a square peg trying to fit into a round hole, and these people made it an easy fit.

I enjoyed myself, though I have politely turned down subsequent offers from my friend to go back.

I'm glad I went.

I learned once again that labels are never a fair judge of who we are.

Whether you are a city slicker or a red neck, odds are that you are simply a person who works hard and enjoys spending your free time hanging out with people who share some common thread with you.

But I do hope that next year, my daughter finds another way to celebrate her birthday.

I'm much too old to be closing down bars with a bunch of red necks.

Just A Thought

Engaging the Next Century

As we approach the year 2000, everybody seems to be looking back at the last century.

We have stories of the greatest athletes, people, events, inventions, teams, movies – there is probably someone out there doing a story on the 50 best commercials, the 50 most beloved animals or the 50 greatest Frat parties of the century.

We've got 'em all folks!

I feel that this exercise in perception is all pretty much unnecessary.

After all, what has happened over the past 100 years has already happened and how we rank them will not change anything.

What's done is done, I always say.

Oh sure, I'm just upset because they didn't even mention Sherman Moffitt in their 50 greatest athletes. I promise you nobody brought more fear to a little league ballpark than my big, powerful, gentle friend Sherman. How well I remember wetting my pants when he stepped into the batter's box, praying that he would not hit another one of his rockets my way. He was an intimidating figure in a league where the rest of us usually had sore arms from holding up our oversized mitts for seven innings.

I vow never to watch ESPN again for excluding the man who, by 5th grade, was known as Sherman Tank.

Michael Jordan was a wimp compared to the Tank, I promise you that.

Be that as it may, I still think looking back on what has been is nowhere near as challenging as looking forward to what might be.

I had a great time as a teenager in the sixties, but have no desire to stand around talking about it much today.

When my daughter tells me how great her 311 concert was, I don't counter with that boring, "when I was your age I went to see Jimmy Hindrix – now that was rock n roll, baby".

Though I certainly appreciate the lessons we can learn from understanding our history, I'm much more interested in looking forward at the possibilities of the history yet to be created.

So I will not bore you with my opinions as to what has been.

I would much rather bore you with my thoughts of what I think might be.

What will be the biggest stories of the next century?

To begin with, the obvious.

The American League will finally realize that baseball was meant to have pitchers in the batter's box and stop the madness of prolonging washed-up player's careers with their

DH crap. The strategy of bunting, sacrificing and negotiating lineup cards is as much a part of baseball as the home run.

But that's a no brainer.

Everybody knows that one except the idiots who hold a position that can actually do something about it.

I'll dig a little deeper.

As I look ahead, I think there are two stories that will have great impact on us during the next century.

First, I have long thought it was pretty lame of us to think that we were the only show in town – and quite egotistical, if I may say so.

I think the time is drawing near when we will finally have to admit that we are not alone in the universe. With all the solar systems, planets, stars and what-not that they are finding out there, I think it just makes sense that they will find life on some other planet.

But the big story will not be in finding life on other planets, but in what we do with this knowledge.

How will this new neighbor affect us?

It is truly an intriguing probability that I hope I'm around to see.

The other story will be the exciting developments in the genetic research already going on.

Cloning sheep and busting criminals from DNA is just the tip of the iceberg, my friends.

By the end of the next century, the list of diseases and

human frailties that potentially could be extinguished will be incredible.

And the quality of life coming from understanding the very roots of our genetic makeup will be astonishing.

Of course, there is a down side to everything that comes in the name of progress.

But I have always been a strong believer in the goodness of the human spirit.

Whatever challenges we face, we have always done so with a core foundation of wanting to do what is right and will be of benefit to all.

And on a personal note, the saddest story of the next century will come about a year after I leave this planet.

Someone will be going through all my writings and say the words a writer dreads to hear, "Gee, that Andy really could write".

A writer seldom gets his due recognition until after it no longer really matters.

After all, what should I expect from a world that couldn't even recognize Sherman Moffitt's impact on the 20th century?

Just A Thought

A Ringing Question

I have often thought that when I die and go to my eternal reward, such as it may be, I'm going to have a lot of questions to ask God.

You know, important questions that never seem to get any answers.

What exactly did Billy Joe Macalister throw off the Tallahassee Bridge?

Is there really life on other planets, and if so, do they all really wear the same drab outfits?

Have you seen Elvis, lately?

Important stuff like that.

But for me, the most important question will be, "What did teenage girls do before Alexander Graham Bell came along?"

For those of you who get irritated by salesmen who call you conveniently at supper time, or those of you who live in horror every time the phone rings with another bill collector demanding your money that you simply do not have, take heart in knowing that your problem is easily solved.

Have a teenage daughter around the house and these little mouthy annoyances will never get through.

Now I fully admit that I am but a lifetime member of the Y- chromosome society.

I have accepted the reality that, no matter how much I may try, I will never understand this female fascination with Ma Bell.

I lost my first girl friend in high school because of the phone. She insisted that I call her each and every night, and I paid a heavy price the next day if I did not follow through.

But hey, I was a stupid teenage boy.

I didn't know any better.

I spent every idle minute at school with her and reserved Friday and Saturday nights for her dating pleasures. That left the week nights for hanging out at the beach with my buddies and Sunday night to catch up with all my homework.

A fair schedule I thought, that provided ample time for all the big ticket items in my life.

But she insisted on the phone call every night, and for awhile, I did the best I could.

The longest day of your life is the thirty minutes you spend on the phone with your girlfriend. You're killing yourself trying to come up with some conversation that you haven't already covered several times during the day, while your body is aching to hit the door and head for the beach. And after fumbling through an eternity of silence, your girlfriend tearfully comes on and proclaims that the relationship is dying, because, "We can't even talk on the phone anymore."

Teenage boys just never get it.

It's not a matter of whether you hold her hand, take her to the right movies, eat lunch with her every day at school, or how fancy a car you may drive.

The absolute basis for a successful relationship with a teenage girl will always be your ability to hold a conversation on the phone with her for 30 minutes each and every day.

Some things are sacred, and for the teenage girl, the telephone is without peer.

I thought I had that part of my life behind me until recently.

God, in her great wisdom, provided me with three daughters.

Three ladies that I love more than life, which are now crashing in on the teenage era of their existence.

And as if to be punishing me for something I did in my youth, God has made one of them a telephone teenager.

I laid down the rule that all conversations could only last ten minutes.

That was a joke.

After each ten-minute conversation, there would be a ten second pause, before the phone rang out and another ten minute conversation would begin.

I am convinced that God is a female!

I've had many father-daughter talks with her about this and have come away from them more confused than ever before.

An adult's common sense approach to things can never

compete with a teenager's line of logic... especially when it is a teenage girl being challenged about her telephone usage.

Women I know laugh at me when I tell my horror stories of my telephone teenager.

Men just cringe in disbelief.

I'm not sure if Alexander Graham Bell had any teenage daughters around when he invented the telephone.

I'm sure he never realized how his invention, more than any other invention, would do more to confuse and leave hopeless the male ego as it tries to win over the better half.

I do know that God and I have a lot to talk about.

Actually, I think my first question will be, "You don't have any phones up here, do ya?"

And if his name is Miss God, I'm dead meat, mister.

Just A Thought

All We Are Say'n

First I must set the record straight.

I was a teenager during the '60s.

I had way too much fun as a teenager during the '60s.

I could tell some stories.

But as I get older, I truly am one older guy who has no desire to talk about the past.

I never want to be the old man who starts every sentence with; "Well, back when I was ...." I don't talk about my past unless someone asks me about it (and SURPRISE: nobody does!).

I'm busy trying to keep up with today.

I'm trying to look forward not backwards.

I say this because an ironic occurrence has occurred to me that makes me chuckle a bit.

The more I ponder the meaning of life in my aging mentality, the more I start humming old '60s songs.

How odd.

This little ball we all hang out on goes through many cycles, stages and eras. As you get older – if you have paid any attention at all to the world you live in – you start to formulate your own ideas about what this whole existence is all about.

I have reached that stage in my life where I have become very comfortable in the philosophy my heart has developed through my experiences.

Life is simple.

We complicate it far too much, but truth is – it's very simple.

You can take all those goofy cookie-cutter phrases and sayings that show up in your inbox every day because someone actually believes a miracle is going to happen to them because they just sent it to you and 12 other sorry saps and pretty much delete them.

They are not the answer.

My approach to life has become simplified into one word; LOVE

You can argue all you want about churches, religions and all, but the answer really is quite simple; you want to get close to God?

Well, God is Love

So if you decide to make everything you say or do the loving thing to say or do, then you will grow close to God.

End of story.

What is the loving thing to say in this situation?

What is the loving action I can take at this moment?

If your focus is all things Love, then your focus is all things God.

That approach will not only become a religious foundation for you, but it will build your foundation for everything you do.

The world is full of complex questions but they all have one answer.

Love.

No matter what issue you throw at me, I guarantee you my answer will be, "What is the loving way to handle this?"

There is a lot of negative energy in this world and a lot of people making a fortune selling books telling us what the formula is for finding true happiness.

I just gave it to you for free in two pages.

Follow Love and find God – period!

All I am saying is give peace a chance.

All you need is Love.

Oh, my God, here comes those '60s songs again!

I wasn't much into the hippie movement of the '60s.

I spent most of that time playing in the wonderful playground called the Pacific Ocean. Sitting on my surfboard checking out the babes along the beach waiting for the next wave was about as philosophically deep as I got.

But as I grow into the twilight of my being, I have to admit that maybe the Peace, Love and Hippies movement wasn't all that bad an idea.

They get no style points to be sure, but I'm definitely giving kudos for substance.

During a time when America threw up as a country, these

flower-powered hippies had a soft voice of love and peace through all the turmoil.

Maybe we should have paid more attention to their message instead of their presentation?

All you need is love, sweet love, love is all you need.

Who'd a thunk John Lennon would be the great philosopher of our time?

Well, not me for sure – but his songs had message ... the right message.

Peace on you!

Just A Thought

Wasteful World of Words

I have become quite concerned recently about how wasteful we have become.

We waste our money, gas, electricity, water, and time.

Why they even tell me that we are now wasting our waste… we are very wasteful with our trash.

But the most wasteful of the wastes is words.

We waste far too many words.

I was reading a story the other day about a committee that sent out a memo to all the baseball owners regarding a possible lockout of spring training.

That sounds okay, except that this alleged memo was 26 pages long.

What makes this even more interesting is that it took only three paragraphs for the news media to explain to us what the 26 pages said.

I'm sorry folks, but for me a memo is one of those little pieces of paper that comes across your desk that reminds you of something you'd sooner forget.

And if it takes the boss 26 pages to do so, then the dear guy is in desperate need of a week at the beach.

The government is easily the worst abuser of words.

Every day a new government report comes out saying very little in 50000 words or more.

This wordy waste dilemma includes volumes of paper piled high on tables in the Senate chambers that says that some committee did not find enough information to make a recommendation on some issue.

It's almost become trendy to write things in volume.

Lawyers make a very good living taking a simple idea and twisting it into a tangled mass of words that only another lawyer could understand ... I believe that's called job security.

Go ahead, look over any legal document you have, and you'll see what I mean.

Even your last will becomes an ocean of nonsense that only a lawyer could understand.

I don't know, to me a Last Will should be pretty straightforward and to the point.

When I die, I know that I can't take everything with me, so I just write down who gets what and let them worry about it.

I might even through in a cute little piece of philosophy about this grand trip through life that I might be remembered by.

But in order to make it legal, I have to have it drawn up by a lawyer... who proceeds to take my little shopping list and turn it into two 11×17 pages of garblie-goop phrases and nonsense in the smallest print available that will leave my poor beloved survivors not knowing anything of what I had in mind for them.

Being a wordsmith who loves to dance my way through a blank piece of paper with this crazy assemblage of letters, I am very hopeful that this trend reverses soon before we get so carried away that we create a paper Babylon.

I think we should all campaign hard to keep our memos, reports, Last Wills and divorces simple and to the point.

Rebel against anything that has to do with volume writing.

If they can't put it down on paper in an easily understood manner, send it back and tell them to try again.

We have created fast food, microwaves, express lanes and instant everything.

Could it be that all these quickie inventions have only made matters worse by giving us more time to write our memos?... God forbid.

Let's spend more time cooking and less time abusing our wonderful world of verbiage.

Of course, this message comes to you by a writer of songs who learned how to tell a complete love story in fifty words or less.

But still...

Just A Thought

Un - Common Misery

The notion of being older but wiser doesn't really impress me all that much now that I'm, well- older.

The older one gets, the more experiences one has which do not increase your intellect as much as it increases your common sense, which we all agree that common sense is always wiser than intellect.

I'm in my 50's right now and I can tell you that I certainly do not think I am more intellectual than I was in my youth, which is also not very impressive given the academic resume of my youth.

But my common sense has increased ten fold as I join the ranks of senior discounts.

A good example of this happened to me this week.

I can tell you with absolute certainty that the person who coined the phrase 'common cold' was in his twenties.

I know this not by reading books or becoming an intellectual genius, but because I am in my fifties and want to find this person and slap him silly for saying such a thing.

When you are in your teens or twenties and catch a cold,

you are likely to simply scoff at it as a mere inconvenience. You continue on with your daily adventures with the only difference being that you are a bit snotty, tend to sneeze more and you hear people say, 'Dude, you sound like ya gotta cold or somethin' – to which you brush them off with an intellectual response that salt water is the perfect cure for the common cold, so let's blow the afternoon classes and go surfing.

When you are in your thirties and forties and catch a cold, you are smart enough not to skip work and go surfing as it has always been hard to sell employers on the benefits of salt water for the common cold.

The cold is more of an annoyance than inconvenience, and you are likely to take a day off from work in the best interest of not spreading germs to your co-workers – and go shopping and running errands as a cold shouldn't stop you from that and how cool is it when you get to Saturday feeling much better and have all those errands taken care of so you can now go to the beach!

Having a cold in your thirties and forties can actually be a nice break for you.

Your spouse, kids and co-workers all feel sorry for you, and don't think for a moment that there isn't one soul alive who doesn't take advantage of this scenario.

We all know how to use the common cold to get us out of many of life's chores.

When you are over fifty, there is nothing common about catching a cold.

Simply put, you want to die.

You force yourself to get out of bed around noon and go lie on the couch.

This gives you a sense of actually doing something.

You might turn on the TV, but your brain is in no condition to even try and comprehend daytime television, so you're better off leaving your world quiet and still.

You stare blankly out your window, as your biggest achievement is in using your eyebrows to lift your heavy eyelids when you occasionally blink.

You want to sleep but it's the middle of the day and after all, this is just a common cold for crying out loud.

Your mind is debating back and forth on whether it's starve a cold, feed a fever or feed a cold, starve a fever.

It doesn't matter however, because the kitchen is well over five feet away and there is no way in hell you are ever going to make that journey.

The hardest part of a common cold after fifty is not the physical, but the emotional beating you take.

You are constantly reminding yourself that this is just a cold as your mind plays back those days of surfing and laughing through this very same disease.

You ponder the paranoia in thinking that if a common cold can reduce you to hours upon hours of glazed staring, what could possibly happen if you actually got sick with something that is not considered common.

When you finally go back to work, you never tell people that you had a cold.

These people are younger than you and will just laugh, so you call it something like bronchitis and try to make it sound like you are a gallant warrior for surviving.

Yes my heightened common sense clearly dictates that those who refer to it as a common cold are too young and stupid to have any say in the matter.

I must stop here.

My eyebrows are exhausted from holding up my eyelids through all of this and I desperately need a nap.

I'm only on day four of this common cold.

Somebody just shoot me already.

Just a Thought

Marketing Apathy

There is one area of our lives that has become far too annoying to me.

It is the one area that has truly lost control.

Not only has it lost control, but I fear that there is no one who is doing anything about it.

It's going to get a lot worse before it gets better.

I'm talking about marketing.

I am certain that the first lesson that a college student will learn when they proclaim Marketing to be their major is the marketing motto.

WE DON'T CARE!

They live by their motto friends, and anything you have to say will gleefully be met by their smirkie smile that shouts their motto.

Let me give you some examples.

One of the trendy marketing tools on the internet right now is the flashing banner. You click on a story you want to read and are greeted by this banner that flashes at a seizure pace that is so annoying, you often forget about the story you wanted to read as you scramble to get out of that page. In fact, the Internet is crawling with annoying marketing practices that pushes many of us to the brink of insanity. Between the pop-up windows, flashing banners and scrolling marquees, it is becoming more and more difficult to find actual beneficial material on any web site.

Most of it is covered with marketing crap.

Marketing Response: WE DON'T CARE!

E-mail has become a dumping ground for many of our marketing friends. It's the same principal as the junk mail we have to gather from our mailbox and throw into the trash every week.

We NEVER ask for it, and have to jump through so many hoops to get the damn thing stopped that most of us just go through the daily ritual of throwing and deleting away these annoying little invasions into our lives.

Of course, we all are greeted around six o'clock every evening by telemarketing fools who know you are about to sit down to dinner, yet actually think that their fiberglass siding is more important than a nice hot meal with the family.

And now they have created automated dialers that spit out these calls at such an amazing pace that a business can annoy 1000 people every evening with just eight people sitting at a phone bank.

Marketing Response: WE DON'T CARE!

The truth is that Marketing people are taking over our world.

Our favorite sports are succumbing to this takeover to

the point that some day soon, every sport will look like NASCAR.

In fact, every industry is being slowly overrun by marketing people.

It's all about marketing strategies that make no effort to consider quality, courtesy or decency.

What is sad is that marketing – when done right – can be a great tool.

I certainly need to market my talents as a writer if I want to get ahead.

The difference between me and the Marketing people is that I care about my product and the people I market my material to.

Sure, I could turn my material over to some marketing agency and make a ton of money.

But I don't have the heart to do so.

I care too much about people.

Here's how it works: You make 100 calls, annoy and piss off eighty people who simply hang up on you. But you get twenty people who actually don't hang up on you. Out of those twenty, you might get five who will actually listen to your script enough to warrant sending them your neat little, no-obligation package, to which you might just get a sale.

Marketing people think this is great stuff.

Make 100 calls and get a sale!

A public relations guy like myself looks at it quite differently.

Annoy and piss off 80 people so you can sell one person something they probably don't even really need?

Only an idiot would think that's a good idea.

Marketing response: WE DON'T CARE.

This is an argument I will never win.

No matter how much we complain, scream, protest or yell, marketing people will always stand true to their motto.

They just don't care.

Just A Thought

Full Moon Rising

Anyone who knows me knows that I'm a big fan of nature.

Not that I'm signing up for the next expedition to the North Pole – no thanks – but I'm always aware of the nature around me and have written several stories about the wonders of this great world we live in.

There has never been any question in my mind that God is the greatest artist of all.

I also contend passionately that anyone who says they do not believe in God is a person who does not observe the nature around them.

Whether I'm standing in the grocery store parking lot watching the clouds mix with the sunshine after a spring storm, taking a moment from my busy day to stand and watch the sparkle of the stars on a cold winter's night, or sitting on the beach watching the Sun dip into the ocean, there is no doubt in my mind that the greatest gift we have is the wonderful changes, cycles and behaviors of nature that constantly amaze those of us who pay attention.

I am one guy who can never get enough of nature's ongoing show time.

Another tidbit about me is that I am a very light sleeper.

I almost always surface from slumber land in the middle of the night and it usually takes me about a month to get back to sleep.

I know they have doctors and pills who can fix this, but for me it's really not a big deal.

That's just who I am.

That's why I was great doing the middle of the night feedings when my girls were infants and that's why I was so awful a human being when I worked the night shifts hey, if I'm a light sleeper in the quiet still of the evenings, how the hell do you expect me to handle sleep during the bright busyness of the daytime?

I was foolish for thinking I could handle that job, but that's another story.

So here I am last night stumbling out of bed about three in the morning much like a pinball bouncing it's way through the obstacles on its way to the home base, colorfully breaking the quiet still of night with several loud thuds and appropriate commentary you wouldn't want your mother to hear, making my way to the bathroom.

My next home must have a direct route from bed to bathroom, that's all I'm saying.

I'm sitting there recovering from my journey when I notice how light it is in my bathroom.

I rub the coma out of my eyes and gaze out my window

where I find the biggest, fullest full moon I've ever seen peeping in on me.

The site really opened my eyes and brought me to reality more than a bucket of cold water dumped over my head.

As if I was looking out during a dark, cloudy day, I could make out every detail of the sleeping night.

I stood and stared out my window for a bit, watching the quiet creek gently rolling by, the trees softly rustling in the breezes of early Fall and the details of each crater on the moon so clearly defined.

I was embraced by the stillness and quiet of such a scene.

As I made my way back to bed, I remember thinking how unfair it is that we humans have to leave this world every night in order to recharge our batteries.

We miss so much of the wonders of God's creativeness every time we close our eyes and call it a day.

I wondered how many people woke up this morning unaware of the extraordinary exhibit of Gods creation they missed during their slumbering rejuvenation?

I wondered how many people working the night shift were sensitive enough to appreciate the special presentation of God's art work?

People often associate the full moon with bringing out the wackiness of others. I take no position on that, but I think it's sad that we miss the real point of a full moon.

For those who are sensitive to the nature around them, the full moon is another great example of the wonderful cycles, beauty and movement in God's creation.

It reassures us of the greatness of God's work and provides comfort in knowing that regardless of the road we travel, God is always close to us.

The more you observe nature, the more you understand how God is always with us.

I'm glad I had to go to the bathroom last night, but I also think it stinks that our bodies have to give up eight hours of every day just to recharge.

You'd think God would have given us a twenty-four hour battery or something.

But as a man who is very sensitive to the nature around me, I know better than to question the artist.

I'm just a little grumpy this morning. I would have truly enjoyed being able to take a chair out by the creek last night and quietly watch the wonderful presentation, but my battery was pretty low, dammit!

Just A Thought

Institutions of Broken Hearts

We are a world built of institutions.

By definition, institutions are important organizations or long held laws or practices.

You have institutions in religion, government, sports and communities.

Marriage is an institution and so are the ducks at the Peabody Hotel.

When something is an institution, you have to respect it.

You don't have to belong to it, but you have to respect the institution.

Institutions identify us.

The institutions that we belong to go a long ways in determining who we are as a people and as an individual.

You can't go through life without being a part of some institution.

I bring this up because lately two of my most favorite institutions I belong to have weighed my heart heavy with sadness.

I'm a baseball nut.

I love baseball season and I love everything about the game of baseball. My daughters can attest to the number of times they were greeted at the breakfast table with, "Today's the most important day of the year!" Of course they politely rolled their eyes over their corn flakes with a muddled, "Something about baseball, right Pops?"

But lately, the headlines have been dominated by players who don't respect the institution of baseball.

A-Rod, Manny, Clemons and Bonds.

Players who put themselves above the game.

They cheat, they lie and then they expect us to feel sorry for them when they are caught.

But they don't respect the institution.

I'm also a Catholic.

Once again, the headlines reflect people in the church who don't respect the institution.

They cheat, they lie and they expect us to feel sorry for them when they are caught.

But they don't respect the institution.

My heart is broken over all this negative debating created from these people. I just want to crawl into a cave and beat my head against a wall every time I hear another commentary about the pathetic state of my chosen institutions that I love so much.

I don't want to debate the issues.

I have no desire to listen to those who wish to use these incidents to prove their fallibility.

The good that comes out of this is that these headlines and

heartaches make you pause and ask yourself a very important question;

So why do you stay?

I'm a Catholic because no other church celebrates the life of Jesus better than the Catholics do every Sunday at Mass.

As long as there is a Catholic Church where I can go to Sunday Mass every week, I will always be a Catholic.

There will likely always be Priests, Nuns, Bishops and even Popes who will show they don't respect the institution, but I'm not a Catholic because of them – I'm a Catholic in spite of them.

I'm a baseball fan because nothing draws me back to my youth more than watching a game of baseball and remembering how I could have turned that play even better when I was a kid.

The older I get, the more I need baseball.

No matter how many players show disrespect for the game, I will still go to ball games.

I don't go for the players, I go for the game.

Institutions are a good thing. We need to be involved with the institutions that identify us most.

But these institutions can and will break our hearts from time to time.

It's important for us to remember that it's never the institution that fails us, but the people who use the institution to better their own lot in life with no respect for the institution they serve.

We, the decent people who do things the right way, will always have to deal with the cheaters who break our hearts.

Right now, it sucks to be a Catholic baseball fan.

But I'm still going to the game Friday night and Mass on Sunday morning.

Then I'll crawl back into my cave and beat my head on a wall for another week.

Just A Thought

A Vote for Reform

So where's the politician when you really need one?

Every year these ambitious people hit the campaign trail, and every year they all stand up for every issue except the one that they need to the most.

The one issue that glares at them every election – right in front of their noses.

And they never do a thing about it.

When will the politicians wise up and put together some election reforms that make since?

How crazy does it have to get before they do something about it?

We had an election here in my town recently that really brought home the problem.

There were three guys running for something called the Juvenile Court Clerk.

I don't know, this doesn't sound like the kind of job that will have a major impact on my community, so I checked it out.

It turns out that this is not the kind of job that will have a major impact on my community.

This person will be responsible for making sure the juvenile court system runs smoothly. Fines are being paid, schedules are being kept, you know that sort of thing. A necessary job certainly, but not one that will make or break a community.

The price tag for doing this work?

Around $35,000 a year... a fair wage for a title that has juvenile in it.

Now the problem that I have with all this is that these three guys who are running for this job are projected to be spending close to $200,000 in posters, flyers, billboards and commercials!

Now folks, that's nearly seven years in salary just to get the job for four years when they will have to spend another $200,000 to keep.

What is wrong with this picture?

And this insanity in budgetary baffleness goes all the way up to the White House!

A candidate for the Presidency will spend millions of dollars to get into the White House... a job that pays a cool $500,000 a year currently ... and is for four years.

Think about it.

How many of you have spent more money getting your job than you will ever receive working the job itself?

It sounds crazy doesn't it?

No wonder these people are having a tough time getting

a handle on our deficit problems! Hey we're talking about people who will spend a fortune to get a job that has a moderate salary and is only good for four years... then they will have to spend another fortune to keep the job another four years.

And we want them to balance our budget?

Let's throw away all the rules and write some new ones before these elections get totally out of control.

Here's some of my ideas...

1- A campaign may not spend in excess of one year's salary of the office that the person seeks... If you want to be the President, you can only spend $500,000 – Period.

2- A campaign may not hire any advertising/PR firm to develop an 'image'...People don't want a fancy Hollywood production with lots of cosmetics and very little substance. They just want to know what each candidate is going to do when they get into office.

3- TV stations will be required to carry programs at no cost to the candidates that will present an overview of each candidate, their background, their views and what they see for the future. Let's get rid of these expensive, cutesy commercials that are short on what THEY will do and long on why voting for the other guy is a vote for Satan!

4- All candidates will have two weeks after the election to remove all their posters, billboards, flyers and stickers from all public and private property. Haven't we all had enough of all these posters that clog our roadsides weeks after the election is decided? And most of these candidates spent a lot of time telling us that they would be environmentally tough? Get outta here!

5- All commercials will have to go through and be approved by the FCC truth in advertising committee and will not be aired until approved for honesty in Content. Aren't we tired of blatant lies in political advertising!

Let's get a handle on these elections America!

They have become nothing more than fancy productions where money and marketing win over substance and sincerity.

Let's move back towards what our forefathers had in mind for a country of opportunity for all... not just for the one with the biggest 'war chest'.

It just might be that if we can make since out of our election process we might just find some politicians that can make since out of our budget deficits.

Just A Thought

Tech This

Okay, so I've spent most of my holiday season playing with all my gadgets and programs that has elevated us into a hi-tech society.

I've been scanning pictures like a mad man.

Creating calendars for my family.

Recording music for my own catalog.

All through this wonderful invention that we have become so dependent on – the PC.

Now keep in mind that we are talking about a guy who is technologically challenged without question. I am one son whose mother never had to concern herself with having me tested to see if I was 'gifted'.

I am not.

Some of you will look at this agenda and think, "What a fun way to spend a holiday".

I only take pleasure in knowing that I live alone and that it was only God in His unending mercy and compassion, that had to hear my four-letter editorials blasting from my mouth as I sloshed through the maddening tasks of modern technology that we are so quick to embrace.

I have broken one chair, put a nasty dent in one microphone, nearly smashed my legendary guitar, sat in amazement that my printer is still talking to me after the left hook I gave it earlier, and I won't even talk about the layers of spit dripping from my monitor, the result of a frenzied lunatic who should know better than to take on projects with such limited mastery.

So today I woke up with a fresh determination to redeem myself.

I was not going to let these modern machines of emotional destruction get the best of me.

No sir, today I would establish without a doubt why I am higher up on the food chain than these machines of metal and wires that we pompously proclaim to not be able to live without.

I got my cup of coffee, sat down to my computer and proceeded to do what I do best.

I wrote stories.

I dusted off some of those creative ideas that have been lurking in my mind for some time and simply wrote stories.

What a great feeling it was too.

My fingers were flying over my keyboard.

I literally had to get up and walk around the house to calm myself down, I was so giddy with celebration at what a genius I had become.

It was statement day for the old man as I snarled and snickered at the monitor.

Don't mess with me today, buster, because I can easily turn you off, turn around and stick a piece of paper in my typewriter and still come up with great stuff.

I don't need modern technology today, although I am thankful for spell-check, to be sure.

Oh the freedom!

Oh the absolute ecstasy of the power to overcome.

To get up and jump back on the horse and command it with authority to move onward!

Awe yes, my friends, modern technology certainly had its way with me this past week.

I was broken, beaten, and brought to my emotional knees at the expense of a collection of electronic toys that, in all fairness, do have the potential of making our lives better if you have reached a plateau of IQs typically connected to being a genius.

But today I got the last word and it came in the form of a story.

Because the truth of the matter is that you can invent machines to do most anything, but they will never be able to create and write a good story.

That, my friends, will never require technology.

A good story only requires a fertile mind and creative heart.

And a couple of good fingers to pound the keyboard.

Point .... Set ... Match .... Me!

Just A Thought

The Shame of the Name

The person who said, "What's in a name?" obviously wasn't named Smith.

I mean you can be born with any number of handicaps and expect a reasonable amount of help from society in dealing with it.

But if you are born into this world with a last name of Smith, you can expect to grow up in a world of abusive misunderstandings no matter what community you hang your shingle on.

You don't know what kind of faces I get when I check into a hotel.

And if my wife happens to be with me, I almost always get a smirky smile and devilish, "I understand, uh...Mr. ...SMITH..." with a wink.

People just don't believe me.

I often get an attitude from people that I really don't appreciate. It comes with this glaring look that I really can't stand. They may as well just come out and say... "Mr.

Smith… sure, pal… if you're going to lie about your name, you could at least find a more creative name to lie with."

And then there is always some fool in the crowd who will say, "Smith, huh?… Gee, are you related to Joe Smith?"

These people probably meet someone from New York City and ask them if they know Joe Brown…."Oh, really," they will say, " Gee, he lives right there in New York City and I thought you might know him."

Nobody knows where the name came from.

No one really cares.

It has no identifiable origin.

When you mention your name, no one ever says, "Oh, you must be Irish."

When you're a Smith, no one knows where the hell you came from.

Even after years of research, I still have no idea how I became a Smith.

As far as I can figure it, our colorful family tree became an uneventful Palm tree somewhere around the Civil War. Something about an Irish relative had a bunch of daughters and one of them married a white guy named Smith and her life – and subsequent family tree branches – became a very vanilla tree void of any redeeming personality.

But please don't ask me to explain.

Being that my family has a long tradition of lousy spellers, I suspect someone got tired of trying to spell their name and decided that it was time to become a Smith.

I do know that I am roughly half-Irish and half-Greek,

with many saying that I favor the Greek side of my family very much.

My father's side was the McDunoughs and my mothers side was the Panagiotopulos (which was later shortened when Uncle Hermes became Hermes Pan the Hollywood Choreographer).

So I'm at a loss as to how I became a Smith from that combination.

Being a Smith, you have to work twice as hard as the others do because your name doesn't establish any form of personality that you can build on.

If your last name is O'Brian, Bartkoski, or Hawthorne, you already have personality traits built into your name.

But when you're a Smith, you fall far behind on the personality charts and have to scramble to convince people that, in spite of your name, you really are a unique individual with a much more exciting personality than the name would suggest.

It's tough being a Smith.

Whenever people discuss the problems of the world, you can bet they will say something really offensive like, "The problem with the world today is that it's run by white guys named Smith!"

When I whine about it being unfair, most people blow me off and say something silly like, "Hey, Pal, if the shoe fits wear it."

Will I'm not buying any shoes and will gladly counter,

"Name me one world leader named Smith …. name me one influential white male named Smith!"

There may be a bunch of white men named Smith, but apparently, none of us are doing much and certainly not enough to get credit for all the problems of the world, for crying out loud!

Of course, being a member of the macho fraternity, I am stuck being a Smith no matter how many times I say 'I do'.

Well being that Congress seems to have trouble passing any significant legislation lately, I thought I'd call on them to show their true colors by passing my bill, which includes…

1) Freedom of choice for newlyweds…choose the last name that you want.

2) A 4.2 billion dollar relief fund for creative writers with the last name Smith (hey, this is the government… you always tack on some serious bucks when running a bill past them)

3) A 22% pay raise for congress (Hey, this is congress, you know… if you want to pass a bill quick, tack on a pay raise)

Well I for one am glad that I have been blessed with three young ladies.

Whenever I'm introduced to a new heartthrob, I always start with their last name.

Just A Thought

That's a Wrap

Well that's enough for now.

I have many more columns than this, but I wanted to only share those stories that were generic in nature and reflected some sense of the mind of a Baby-Boomer.

I felt that there was something here for everyone.

Some made you laugh and think that I was a genius.

Others didn't touch a nerve of any kind and made you think I'm an idiot.

It's all good by me.

I have long thought that I am neither a genius, nor an idiot.

I am a writer.

A writer with a lot of thoughts.

It's been my pleasure to share my thoughts with you.

To contact or learn more about the author
You need to go to:

WWW.TKRWRITENOW.COM

CPSIA information can be obtained
at www.ICGtesting.com
Printed in the USA
BVHW070842160919
558543BV00001B/19/P